Return to THE Coca-Cola TRAIL

More PEOPLE and PLACES in the History of Coca-Cola

LARRY JORGENSEN

Published by
Modern History Press
5145 Pontiac Trail
Ann Arbor, MI 48105

info@ModernHistoryPress.com
Tollfree 888-761-6268
FAX 734-663-6861

Contents

Introduction

"Return to the Coca-Cola Trail" is our second journey to visit the places and to discover the histories of the people who played an important role in creating the world's best known product. Like our first trip on the *trail* we'll share many true experiences from the pioneering Coca-Cola bottlers who in the early 1900s saw what they hoped would be an opportunity. That hope combined with dedication and tireless efforts resulted in an amazing new business which would prosper and continue to grow for over 125 years.

"Return to the Coca-Cola Trail" and visit old Coca-Cola plants which have new lives as museums, entertainment centers, shops, gift stores and more. Learn about an internationally famous wildlife artist who was responsible for a change in the familiar Coca-Cola logo. Enjoy the true story of how a small town became famous as the city of Coca-Cola millionaires. Discover why the familiar Coca-Cola glass bottle has a green color tint.

Fascinating historic photos accompany each stop on the *trail*.

Communities across the nation showcase their efforts to save, restore and proudly display their original Coca-Cola murals as an important part of their history.

The business of bottling Coca-Cola changed through the years from over 1200 individual bottlers in the 1920s to less than 100 bottlers a century later. But the visibility and community involvement continue to expand along with modern new Coca-Cola distribution centers.

The well-established traditions of Coca-Cola at Christmas are found everywhere along the *trail*. Coca-Cola exhibits by collectors and fans are frequently displayed.

Coca-Cola is not simply a reliable "old friend," it is generations of history and special memories. It is that search for more memories that create this invitation to join us as we "Return to the Coca-Cola Trail."

Chapter 1
Why Is The Bottle Green?

Why do the traditional Coca-Cola glass bottles have a light green tint?

The color was the unexpected result of a decision by the Coca-Cola Company to seek and establish a distinctive design for their bottle. The soft drink bottling industry was booming in the early 1900s, and with numerous bottlers using similar style bottles, visual confusion was created for the consumer and the industry. It even became possible for one bottler to mimic the appearance of another more successful product.

The Coca-Cola Company announced a plan in 1913 to solve the problem by initiating a competition among bottle manufacturers to design a new and exclusive Coca-Cola bottle. The competition was won by the Root Glass Company of Terre Haute, Indiana and their new, and now famous, bottle design was patented in 1915.

Five years earlier the Root Glass Company had purchased a 160 acre sandstone quarry site called Fern Cliffs, near Greencastle, about fifty miles from their glass plant in Terre Haute. Sandstone is a main ingredient in the glass making process.

Today the Fern Cliffs area is a dedicated state nature preserve, called both a floral paradise and sandstone marvel. Historians believe the cliffs were formed millions of years back, as the shore to a primeval sea. In more

Fern Cliffs

recent history, the Shawnee Indian tribe built a small village at the base of the cliffs. However, in the 1830's U.S. soldiers evicted the Shawnees to make the area more attractive for new white settlers. The site became an early trading post, and later a booming village with stores, a post office and a popular resort.

The site contained an abundance of sandstone for glassmaking, and those early Coca-Cola bottles were made from that sand. The stone was crushed, washed with water from the nearby Snake Creek, and loaded into rail cars to be transported to the Terre Haute plant. A spur line of the New York Central Railway served the quarry operation.

During its heyday as many as twenty men worked at the quarry around the clock to crush and wash the sandstone. Approximately 20,000 tons of sandstone were taken from the site every year.

It was the unique mixture of copper and other minerals in that sand which created the green tinge in the first Root bottles. Coca-Cola was pleased with the result and consequently specified in future bottle production contracts that the bottles include the color tint which was first

Root Glass Company Fern Cliff sand washing/ crushing operation

Photo courtesy of Root Glass Archives

called "German green", but later re-identified "Georgia green" to honor Coca-Cola's home state. When glass plants in other locations were contracted to produce Coca-Cola bottles, minerals would be added, if needed, to achieve the same color as the Fern Cliffs bottles.

The Root glassworks was sold in 1932 to the Owens-Illinois Glass Company. Operations continued at Fern Cliffs for another four years, until a new more pure source of glass sand was located. Owens-Illinois eventually gave the site to the Girl Scouts of Putnam County, for future use as a campground and other scouting activities. Fern Cliffs was designated as a national landmark in 1980, and as an Indiana state nature preserve in 1988 and 1996.

Museum executive assistant Megan Rentfro, shows the bottles which include a Root bottle which was produced for Gardner Brothers Bottling of Greencastle.

A display of old green tinted bottles, made from Fern Cliffs sand, can be seen at the Putnam County Museum in Greencastle.

Coca-Cola was first bottled in Greencastle in 1914 by Otis and Charles Gardner. Records show that first year they used 656 gallons of syrup, which should have produced over 4,000 cases of 6 ½ ounce bottles. They also were bottling an orange cider drink, ginger ale, cream soda, sasparilla, and strawberry soda.

The Gardner brother started out with an ice business in 1905. Six years later they added an ice cream business which had been started in 1895 by their father Josiah. When Gardners purchased the Greencastle Coca-Cola franchise they incorporated under the name Coca-Cola Bottling Company, Inc. The idea for the new venture must have impressed the local business community because Perry Rush, who had been vice president of a local bank for twenty-two years, resigned his bank position to join the Gardners. He became vice president of Coca-Cola Bottling, while Otis Gardner was President and Charles was Secretay-Treasurer. Residents of the Greencastle area responded favorably to the new beverage, and Otis reported the company's success to the local paper on New Year's day, 1929. He proudly boasted that sales the preceding year were "enough to supply 37 bottles of Coca-Cola to every man, woman and child in Putnam County."

The Gardner Brothers played an important role in the history of another Greencastle business, Handy's Dairy. The dairy had recently constructed a new milk production facility when it was destroyed by a fire in 1925. Handy's accepted an offer to continue business in space available at Gardner's ice cream plant, and they operated there for over a year while the destroyed milk plant was being rebuilt. Ironically twenty-five years later, Handy's purchased Gardner's ice cream business and added ice cream and novelty frozen products to their milk delivery business.

It was wartime in 1945, and that summer Otis ran an advertisement in the local newspaper with the heading "refuses sugar substitutes". The ad explained that beginning July 1st there would be an "equitable system" for rationing Coca-Cola in Greencastle.

The ad explained, "we will not compromise the integrity of Coca-Cola with sweetening substitutes." Otis then proudly stated, "we will cooperate with government regulations. We still have a war to win and that comes first!"

The war also did not slow the Gardner brothers enthusiasm for the Coca-Cola business, because in 1945 they announced plans to build a new bottling plant. That building remained after the bottling business was sold, being purchased in 1991 by A. A. Huber for his heating and air conditioning business. A health studio also occupied a portion of the building.

It is interesting to note Greencastle actually was home to two bottling plants for a brief period in the early 1900's. The growing popularity of

the new bottled soda business apparently attracted the interest of George W. Bence, a local doctor and businessman. In 1909 he opened the PleZee Company, and boasted the quality of his beverage with the slogan "Ple-Zee, Best Soft Drink on Earth".

To create attention and creditability for the "best on earth" claim, the company conducted a taste test on a Monon Railroad excursion trip to Michigan City. After the event, PleZee proudly announced the sale of eight cases of soda during the trip. However, records indicate the PleZee Beverage Company survived less than five years. One of many entrepreneurs throughout the country who tried to copy a successful idea, but couldn't match the competition of the light green bottle from Greencastle.

Chapter 2
Atlantic, Iowa

Atlantic is a southwest Iowa farming community which has become recognized for its Coca-Cola heritage and for a popular annual Coca-Cola event.

The Coca-Cola history in Atlantic is the amazing story of an Iowa family whose business interests ultimately lead to the creation of one of the nation's most unique independent Coca-Cola bottlers. It started when a forgotten contract for the bottling of Coca-Cola was discovered in the safe of a newly acquired business. It is the story of the Tyler family.

For over 135 years the Tylers have owned and operated businesses in southwest and central Iowa. It began in Villisca where Frank "Perk" Tyler would cut ice from a river to be stored and later sold to his customers when needed during warmer weather. Frank also became involved in other businesses, including a brick factory, gasoline

Crystal Lake Ice

Clarinda Bottling Works

and kerosene delivery for Standard Oil, and even a lakeside entertainment facility.

The making and selling of ice cream was added to the ice business, and in 1909 Frank sold that business to his three sons; Royal, Harry and Henry. Six years later the sons expanded the business when they began to produce soda drinks, which they called "Tyler's Flavors", a decision which ultimately lead to the creation of a vast and rewarding Coca-Cola enterprise. The Tylers were producing a variety of sodas, including orange, grape, strawberry and root beer. But the idea to bottle Coca-Cola almost came by accident after the 1916 purchase of a creamery in Clarinda, Iowa. Inside the company safe they discovered a neglected franchise agreement to allow the bottling and sale of Coca-Cola.

The Tylers had heard of the success of Coca-Cola in other states, and realized their Iowa customers were not familiar with the new drink. They decided to begin making Coca-Cola. To introduce the new beverage a few bottles were added to each case of their other soda flavors. The demand for Coca-Cola grew. Harry wanted to make cold Coca-Cola available, so he would ask store owners to save the wooden boxes which had been used to ship cheese to their stores. During the winter the boxes were filled with bottles of Coca-Cola and placed on outside window sills.

In 1923 Royal Tyler sold his interest in the business to brothers Harry and Henry, and growth continued. Bottling plants were purchased in Atlantic, Shenandoah and Creston, with Atlantic acquiring the rights to bottle and sell Coca-Cola in 1929. The ice cream business in Clarinda was sold to the Meadow Gold Company in 1930, as the emphasis on Coca-Cola bottling increased with the 1936 purchase of a plant in Grand Island, Nebraska.

The Tyler brothers decided in 1949 to divide the business, and drew straws to determine ownership of each location. The Atlantic and Creston plants went to Harry, while Henry received Shenandoah and Grand Island. Harry's family continued to operate and expand Atlantic bottling, while ultimately Henry's family decided to sell the business in Shenandoah and Grand Island. Harry's son Jim was managing Atlantic Bottling by 1958, and customers were receiving Coca-Cola, 7-Up, and Tyler's Flavors, along with some new brands including Squirt, Dr. Pepper and Frostie Root Beer.

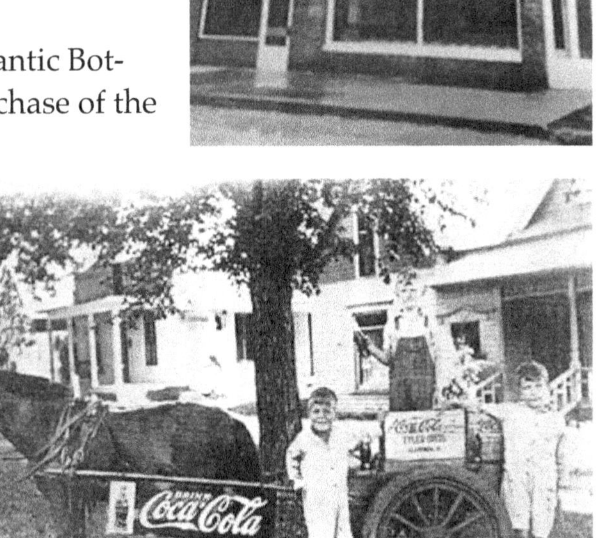

A major expansion for Atlantic Bottling came in 1975 with the purchase of the Des Moines plant and franchise, which added a service area with a population of more than 400,000 residents. Jim Tyler's son Kirk, who was Atlantic Sales Manger, played a major role in the Des Moines acquisition. At that time the plant in Des Moines had stopped bottling and was already obtaining Coca-Cola products

Harry's son Jim with two friends. At the age of 4, he was already promoting Coca-Cola.

from Atlantic. Under the Tyler ownership rapid growth was experienced in Des Moines, with a new sales facility and warehouse being constructed in 1989 in nearby Waukee.

Kirk Tyler became President of Atlantic Coca-Cola in 1991, while his

Jim and Kirk Tyler

father became Chairman of the Board. Jim Tyler was inducted into the Iowa Business Hall of Fame in 2015. Meanwhile growth continued in Des Moines, and a 400,000 sq. ft. building was purchased near the airport in 2016.

Atlantic Bottling's area of distribution expanded again in 2016 when territories acquired from the Coca-Cola Company included six more Iowa locations, as well as the quad cities in Illinois. A new $8 million distribution facility was constructed in Walcott, Iowa to serve the quad-city area.

From a chance contract discovery in a small ice cream plant, what evolved is now Atlantic Bottling, which distributes Coca-Cola products in almost all of Iowa, as well as portions of Illinois, Minnesota, Wisconsin and Missouri. And Atlantic, Iowa remains the center of it all, with all bottling and canning of Coca-Cola products being done at the modern Atlantic headquarters plant.

The community of Atlantic is unique for its enthusiastic support for their local Coca-Cola bottler, and for the development and promotion of one of the nation's largest Coca-Cola events of its kind. It's called "Coca-Cola

Days" which began in 1993 as a chamber of commerce promotion designed to attract visitors and attention for the city.

The Iowa chapter of Coca-Cola collectors enthusiastically became involved that first year, and set up a small swap meet in a vacant downtown building. The event quickly caught the attention of other collectors

and Coca-Cola enthusiasts, and has grown to become the second largest collectors show in the United States.

The 25th anniversary of "Coca-Cola Days" was observed by the chamber of commerce in 2017 when they sponsored an event called "Bottles on Parade." Chamber Executive Director Bailey Smith encouraged local businesses to decorate and display large Coca-Cola bottles. Visitors and shoppers were asked to vote for their favorite bottle creation, with a winner recognized on the opening day of the celebration.

Cappell's Ace Hardware   *Hanson's Fine Jewelry*

Photos courtesy of Cass County Historical Museum

The collectors show was relocated to the large Herring building, an historic structure owned and provided each year by Atlantic Coca-Cola. The building's unique history dates back to pre-Coca-Cola days in Atlantic. Known originally as the Atlantic Automobile Company, it was owned by Clyde Herring and was used for the assembling and sales of Ford model T autos. Herring was born and raised in Jackson, Michigan, where as a young man, he worked in a jewelry store and became acquainted with Henry Ford as he often repaired Ford's watches.

As a result of that relationship Ford gave Herring a free car in 1910 along with the exclusive rights to own Ford dealerships in the entire state of Iowa. In those early auto industry years completed cars would not be shipped. Instead the vehicle's pieces were sent, to be assembled by the dealer. Thus was born the need for Herring's two story Atlantic automobile facility.

Herring's success with the new Ford vehicle came quickly, allowing him to purchase real estate in Des Moines, valued at that time at more than $3 million. By 1915 Herring had sold more cars than any other U.S. Automobile agency. In 1932 he was elected Governor of Iowa, serving two terms before being elected to the U.S. Senate.

Another example of the Coca-Cola pride in Atlantic is the privately owned and operated Coca-Cola Center and Museum, located in a former downtown store building. Owned by local resident and Coca-Cola collector Margaret Slepsky, the

museum is open on weekends and contains a wide variety of historic items, including a display of Coca-Cola bottles from every state. One colorful area in museum features the popular Coca-Cola Christmas and Santa items. Also on display are old soda fountain items, advertising, vending machines, and other memorabilia. Many of the objects have been donated, while others are on loan to the museum.

Margaret Slepsky

The museum was opened in 2009 in a former locker plant, and in 2011 an old Coca-Cola "ghost sign" on the side of the building, was brought back to life by Atlantic artist Connie Boose. The original mural

had been done in the 1940s, and the 2011 painting marked the second time Connie Boose had restored the sign, having first given it a fresh appearance twenty-five years earlier.

Connie, who has a bachelor's degree in art, has done six Coca-Cola murals in Atlantic, as well as outdoor signs in other communities. The museum restoration was her first and that sign and another were donated by the artist. Her work caught the attention of the Tylers at Atlantic bottling and she was commissioned to create four more.

A special memory for Connie is a Sprite Boy mural which she painted in 1998 across from city hall. The Sprite Boy design was said to be a favorite of Mrs. Jim Tyler. Another popular mural is from a World War II poster, which is painted on the Herring building.

Every September the "Coca-Cola Days" event showcases what is a year round appreciation and long time bond between an Iowa community and its popular Coca-Cola bottler. "It's the Real Thing", a refreshing stop on the Coca-Cola Trail.

Chapter 3
Florida Panhandle

The Florida Panhandle, known for its 200 miles of white sand beaches, also contains a wealth of early Coca-Cola bottling history.

Keeping that history alive and available for Coca-Cola fans, collectors, and Florida visitors is the Buccaneer Gift Shop in Fort Walton Beach. Featuring what has been called the largest Coca-Cola memorabilia collection in the southeast, the Buccaneer also is unique as the only place to have your photo taken alongside a 15-foot high Coca-Cola bottle, or to purchase a special custom imprinted bottle of Coca-Cola which commemorates the store's 35th anniversary.

The shop reflects five decades of work and dedication by the Ring family, Oscar and Ann, and their children Jeff and Cheryl. It began in 1972 with three stores in downtown Fort Walton Beach. Along with the Buccaneer there were the Coral Reef and Pelican's Pouch where souvenirs, sea shells, and nautical items were sold.

The business was downsized to one store after Ann died, but the family's emphasis on memorabilia collecting and selling continued to grow. Oscar put thousands of miles on his van as he visited many states

in search of memorabilia for the store. He visited pre-advertised sales and searched for treasures at flea markets and antique stores. Often he was first in line when a new Coca-Cola commemorative bottle was introduced.

The Buccaneer's 15-foot bottle was acquire by the Rings in 2007, after it had been created for a promotion by the Coca-Cola Company. At first Jeff wanted to place the 400-lb fiberglass creation on the roof of his shop. However, to do so would have required special approval by the city council to designate the bottle a "landmark sign". There also was concern about how the bottle would withstand strong gulf winds or a hurricane.

Ultimately the decision was made to position the bottle on a specially constructed raised platform next to the store, where visitors were invited to have their photo taken while standing next to the large one-of-a-kind Coca-Cola bottle.

Jeff Ring with his 15-ft tall Coke bottle.

No doubt the collecting of the various

commemorative Coca-Cola bottles triggered Jeff's desire to have a commemorative bottle created for the Buccaneer. Often he was told it couldn't be done, and he encountered many challenges to his pursuit for that special bottle. It was said that a Coca-Cola bottle for just one store had never been approved by Coca-Cola. Another problem would be to identify the bottle as from Fort Walton Beach, because Coca-Cola had never been produced in that city.

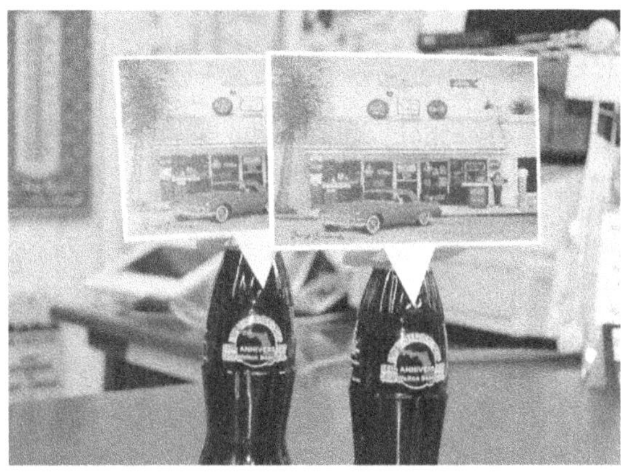

Anniversary bottle with special topper.

Finally, after almost twenty years of chasing his commemorative bottle dream, Jeff's idea became a reality when Coca-Cola agreed to create the unique bottle in December 2007. The Coca-Cola plant in Marietta, Georgia produced what was said to be the smallest possible run of custom imprinted bottles of Coca-Cola. A total of 3,696 bottles were filled.

The bottle features a red and white imprinted logo which commemorates the 35th anniversary of the Buccaneer Gift shop. Jeff was there to watch, as it took only seven minutes of bottling to end his twenty year journey. Collectors had learned of the promised new bottle, and over 900 were pre-sold before being produced.

Fourteen years later only 300 remained available at the Buccaneer. Each bottle is hand numbered on the bottom and sells for $15.00. The first bottle from that production run is proudly displayed as a tribute to persistence, in a glass case at the store.

Collectors of Coca-Cola memorabilia often discover old vending machines. Such was the case for the Rings, but that took them to another business venture; rebuilding and restoring old Coca-Cola machines. Customers would either see or be looking for an old vendor to have restored to working condition. A warehouse building in nearby Gulf Breeze became the site for the restoration work, and over 100 machines were rebuilt

Jeff and Oscar Ring with restored vending machine

before hurricane Ivan destroyed the building in 2004. Their largest machine restoration was done for the Coca-Cola Company and require almost a year to complete. Another customer, who was a dedicated collector, had over 25 old machines restored for his personal collection. The Rings own a 1937 restored vending machine, which is one of only 500 ever made and is valued at over $15,000.

The Buccaneer also has a display of Coca-Cola bottles from the early days of bottling in the Florida panhandle. Coca-Cola was first bottled in 1903 in Pensacola by L. G. Crosby. About two decades later, a warehouse Crosby had established in DeFuniak Springs, was enlarged to provide bottling at that location as well.

In 1915 the plant and Panhandle territory were purchased by Charles Veazey Rainwater, who is recognized in Coca-Cola history as being responsible for much of the early years growth of Coca-Cola bottling. He has been called "Dean of Coca-Cola bottlers".

Rainwater first became involved in Coca-Cola in 1904, just five years after Asa Candler, the owner and manufacturer of the Coca-Cola syrup, authorized the bottling of the beverage. Candler had sold the exclusive rights to bottle to Chattanooga businessmen Ben Thomas and Joseph Whitehead. The two decided to divide their acquired U.S. territory.

Photo courtesy of University of West Florida Historic Trust Collections

Whitehead moved to Atlanta where he established Dixie Coca-Cola Bottling Company, and also sold territory bottling rights to future bottlers. To raise necessary funding for his Atlanta operation, Whitehead had sold half of his share of the business to John Lupton, also from Chattanooga. When Whitehead died unexpectedly in 1906, Rainwater was contacted by Lupton who convinced Veazey to become Secretary-Treasurer of the Atlanta operation. Rainwater was known by Lupton because two years earlier the two men had partnered in establishing a Coca-Cola plant in Athens, Georgia.

The Pensacola plant and territory, was purchased in 1915 by Rainwater and his brother-in-law, J. Henry Edmondson for $400,000. Known as Hygeia

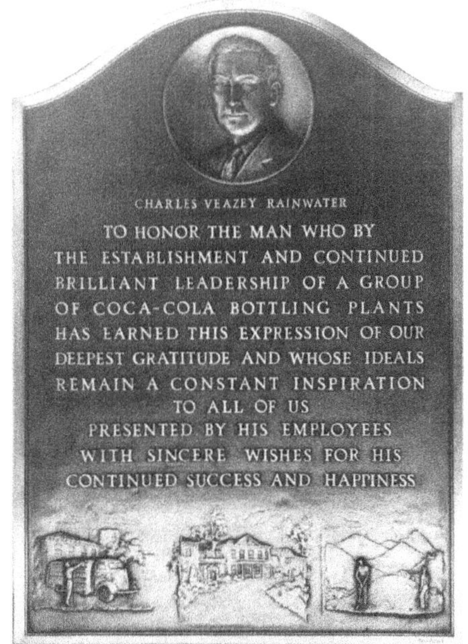

Photo courtesy of University of West Florida Historic Trust Collections

Warehouse in Pensacola. Photo courtesy of University of West Florida Historic Trust Collections

Warehouse in DeFuniak Springs. Photo courtesy of Scott Clary

Bottling Works, Hygeia and Pensacola ultimately became corporate headquarters for Rainwater as additional family owned plants were purchased in Tallahassee; Beaumont and Paris, Texas; Columbia, SC; Swainsboro, GA; and Annisten and Oxford, Alabama.

However, during this time Rainwater also retained his leadership role at Dixie Bottling in Atlanta.

When the Pensacola plant was purchased, Crosby also had expanded distribution with the warehouse in DeFuniak Springs, as well as a second warehouse about 45 miles north of Pensacola at Century, Florida near the Alabama state line.

Both warehouses were located adjacent to rail lines to better accommodate shipments to and from Pensacola.

William G. Wallace was the local manager for the warehouse in DeFuniak Springs, and he personally did most of the product delivery in that area. Wallace remained as manager when Rainwater decided to enlarge the building in 1924 to allow local bottling to begin. The new plant could produce 1200 cases per day, and additional trucks and drivers were required to handle the increased production. Wallace remained with DeFuniak Coca-Cola for over 40 years.

The demand for Coca-Cola continued to grow, and in 1941 a modern new plant was constructed on north ninth street, and remained in operation for 38 years. The building became home for Southern Power Works, which still proudly displays the familiar cast cement Coca-Cola signs on the outside walls. Business owner Terry Waldrop retained the original blueprints of the building and observed that

Southern Power Works in former plant. Photo courtesy of University of West Florida Historic Trust Collections

Pensacola plant building

the old freight elevator still was in working condition. Historic stairs, floors and second floor work areas also remained.

Pensacola became corporate headquarters for all Rainwater family owned plants, and Veazey remained Hygeia President until he retired in 1961. He had selected Pensacola as his primary home in the 1940's. C. Veazy Rainwater died in 1973 at the age of 91. He was born in Veazy, Georgia, a town named after his mother's family.

In the 1980s Coca-Cola Corporation began purchasing various bottling groups to create what would become Coca-Cola Enterprises, a separate entity which was spun off from the company. In October 1986 an agreement was reached for CCE to purchase the Hygeia companies owned by the Rainwater family. A Wall Street Journal report at that time estimated the sale value at over $150 million.

I.V. Rainwater's son, Crawford was Corporate Chairman at the time, and his grandson Jody, was plant manager. There were 311 employees in Pensacola and over 1200 employees throughout the Rainwater companies.

During that time period when Coca-Cola was purchasing bottling groups, they also purchased Lupton's Chattanooga based group for $1.4 billion, and the Beatrice Foods group for $1 billion.

Then in 2007 the Coca-Cola Company changed direction, and began re-franchising the company owned bottling operations, to return the ownership to local partners.

The Pensacola operation was acquired from Coca-Cola Corporate in 2014 by Coca-Cola United of Birmingham. United is the 3rd largest Coca-Cola bottler in the United States, with 54 distribution centers and 9 plants in six southeastern states.

Visitors to the Florida Panhandle who are interested in Coca-Cola memorabilia or other treasures of history, also may enjoy a visit to the Magnolia Grill, another fascinating stop in Fort Walton Beach. Owned by Tom and Peggy Rice, the popular restaurant is affectionately referred to by locals as "the museum that serves meals."

Magnolia Grill

Tom Rice is a dedicated area historian, known for his desire to acquire and preserve items of historical interest, with many of the items prominently displayed throughout his restaurant. If interested in Coca-Cola memorabilia, a diner might be seated next to Tom's Coca-Cola collection, which includes old advertising, crates, an old cooler, various collectibles, and rare old bottles. He even acquired a complete soda fountain when an old local drug store went

Tom Rice with his bottles

out of business. However, that large item is stored with other "treasures" at a nearby warehouse. Items from the warehouse inventory often are borrowed to be used as decorations in local themed events.

Tom's Coca-Cola bottle collection includes rare bottles from Cuba's pre-Castro days, which had been acquired by his grandparents during a vacation trip to the island. Others in his display include a dozen mysteriously acquired bottles from the old plant in DeFuniak Springs. Tom had commented during a local radio show, that he wished he had bottles representing the former plant. The next morning the old bottles, in a brown paper sack, were discovered at his front door. They were packed with sand and dirt, appearing as if retrieved from the nearby bay. Tom had to scrub the bottles and soak them in vinegar for over a week, before adding them to the collection.

A meal at the Magnolia Grill in Fort Walton Beach comes with a "side" of area history, and often a memory shared by Tom Rice.

A new life was assured for the historic Coca-Cola building in Pensacola in the summer of 2020 when the building was purchased by an expanding Pensacola business. Built in 1936 it was the last plant for Hygeia

Coca-Cola and was closed in 1967. The plant sat vacant for several years sustaining water damage and overall deterioration.

"Keep Pensacola Beautiful" attempted to raise money to buy the building in 2019, but dropped their plans when learning the cost to remediate the building was estimated at about $8 million.

The building ultimately was purchased by Industrial Energy Services, a national LED lighting company which had been operating for fifteen years in an industrial park facility and needed additional space for expansion. Company co-owner David Fetter said "despite the age and wear and tear the old Coca-Cola building is truly a remarkable structure with historic value to Pensacola."

The new owners were to restore the building keeping its "architectural elements" as they realized what the structure means to the Rainwater family and the former Coca-Cola employees who worked there.

Chapter 4
Tullahoma, Tennessee

Coca-Cola history is alive and well in Tullahoma, Tennessee thanks to a pioneer family bottler and a local historian who saved an old Coca-Cola plant from destruction.

Coca-Cola was first bottled in Tullahoma in 1906 when Frank D. Tate acquired the territory franchise from Ben Thomas in Chattanooga. After operating his new business for six years, Pate sold to two brothers, Frank and W. D. Medearis.

Seven years later the Coca-Cola plant again changed ownership, and again it was purchased by two brothers, Charles V. and J. W. Holland, whose descendants have continued the Coca-Cola tradition in Tullahoma. Charles and J. W. were the great grandfather and great granduncle of current company President Jordan E. Ennis.

Charles Holland had first become interested in acquire a Coca-Cola plant while living in Alabama, where even during the hard times of World War I, he observed the growth and apparent success of this new beverage. The business in Tullahoma became available, and Charles moved his family there to make the purchase with his brother. However, two years later he became the sole owner when J. W. died. Charles' son-in-law, Jordan G. Ennis assumed control when Charles passed away in 1931, and lead the company through changes and continued

J.W. Holland

growth for the next forty years.

It was during that time the decision was made to build a new state of the art plant, which remains today as an important reminder of Tullahoma's Coca-Cola history.

A site on highway 55 west (the road to Lynchburg) was selected and construction began in February 1941. In just six months the modern new facility was turning out 120

C. V. Holland and John "Doc" Hill with flatbed truck used for deliveries in the 1920s.

bottles per minute, operating 24 hours per day, six days per week. The demand for Coca-Cola was great, as the plant served an area which included 125,000 servicemen and prisoners of war at nearby Camp Forrest, and an additional World War II air pilot training facility.

Proud Coca-Cola owners and employees after new plant is completed in 1941. Standing on the left in back row are John G. Ennis, John Holland, and John "Doc" Hill.

An important factor in selecting the plant's location was an adjacent railroad spur line, as special cases were being used to ship Coca-Cola by rail to distant locations in the Tullahoma territory. That convenience became less important as highways were improved after the war.

A long-time employee, Wesley Davis on the bottling line. More than thirty years later he went on to work at the new plant.

Jordan G. Ennis' son Steven joined the company in 1968 after serving two years in the Army, including 13 months in Korea. He became manager, president, and chairman of the board; and it was during his leadership the current plant was built east of town on highway 55. More products were being bottled and a larger facility would be critical to meet the demand. Bottling at the old plant was discontinued in October of 1973.

Territory expansion also began at that time, with the Coca-Cola plant in McMinnville purchased in 1971. The Tullahoma Dr. Pepper plant was purchased from J. C. Morgan in 1973, and his son Jeff Morgan became Vice President of Dr. Pepper operations at the new Coca-Cola plant. A Coca-Cola operation in Shelbyville was purchased in 1982, followed by a large acquisition in 1987 when both the Coca-Cola and Dr. Pepper lines were purchased from Clarksville.

A name familiar to many

Memories of the old Coca-Cola plant were preserved with this sign. The large cement logos were removed from the old building and used to create this unique identification at the front of the new plant.

Coca-Cola collectors and fans, Elizabethtown, Kentucky, was the territory purchased in 1999 by Tullahoma. At one time Elizabethtown was home to the world's largest private collection of Coca-Cola memorabilia. The famous Schmidt museum was the result of a collecting obsession by Bill and Jan Schmidt, who also operated the local Coca-Cola business. Over 80,000 items were included in an auction when their museum was closed in 2012.

Coca-Cola fans will find a visit to the Tullahoma plant worthwhile, as the Company Store, located next to the bottling plant, displays and sells a wide variety of Coca-Cola products. From collectibles to decorations and clothing items; more proof that Coke is the most sought after product name in the world

The Coca-Cola theme is continued in the plant's private offices, including a lobby display of an old-fashioned soda fountain.

When Tullahoma Coca-Cola observed its' centennial year of service in 2006, it was noted the company was providing service to an area including over three-quarters of a million consumers, in 30 counties in Tennessee and Kentucky.

Jorden E. Ennis became President and CEO when his father Steven

died in 2012. The company remains unique as a local independent, operating a modern bottling line. The plant bottles 20 ounce carbonated beverages and 2 liter bottles. It also bottles Dasani water using a reverse osmosis process which purifies Tullahoma water to a minimal 1-percent of sediment. So pure, is the claim, the final product won't "even conduct electricity". The Dasani water produced in Tullahoma is distributed in all Tennessee markets except Memphis and Chattanooga.

Not gone and not forgotten! That's the status of the old Tullahoma Coca-Cola building, thanks to the unique dedication and years of hard work by a local historian who saved the plant from demolition.

When bottling was moved from the old plant, the building was used for a few years for a vending machine business. Then it sat empty until June 2000 when it was purchased by Russell Credle, a Tullahoma

native, who had developed an interest in area history as a child, while exploring the old Camp Forrest Army site. The Coca-Cola building brought back many memories for Russell and he was determined to restore the aging structure while, at the same time, maintaining a full time job which required he be out of state five days a week.

Working on weekends and during vacations for nearly four years, Credle was able to achieve, through his own efforts and talent, 90-percent

of the required
restoration work.
He termed it a labor
love which provided
an opportunity to
learn how to do
things he had not
done before.

He remodeled
the upper level into
a comfortable apart-
ment where he lived
for nine years. The
unique living space
was included in the city's 2002 tour of homes.

Credle admits the project turned out to be larger than he anticipated
as he had to replace the large windows, plumbing, electrical, nine heating
and air units, and much more. However, he said "it was one of the most
rewarding things I've ever done."

Not only did he restore the building, he can be credited with saving
it. Credle learned if the building had not been sold, there were plans to
donate it to the
local Motlow State
Community College,
and the college
would have had the
building torn down
to utilize the site for
another purpose.

The old Coke
building evokes
special memories
for many in the

community. At one time a large upstairs hall was used for high school dances. That memory was renewed again in 2006 when a class reunion was held in that same hall, with catering provided by the fifties style restaurant below. And like many Coca-Cola plants, there were the fascinating visits to watch the bottling. The building took on another community role, when during the war, it was designated an approved bomb shelter.

Tenants began leasing space in the building soon after the renovation was completed in 2004. Now known as the "Shoppes at Cokers," included are a cafe in the former bottling area in front, and unique shops in the mini-mall behind. Coca-Cola signs and memorabilia are displayed throughout.

The half-million dollar restoration has been featured on television and in publications, including Southern Living Magazine, which called the project an "incredible renovation." Credle was honored in 2011 as the area's "Businessman of the Year".

Russell Credle with a few of his old advertising signs.

Credle's love of history extends beyond his restored building, as he also saves old advertising signs, which of course, include the often sought Coca-Cola signs. His collection, said to be one of the largest in the area, is displayed in a large barn style structure he constructed near his home. People fascinated by old signs and history often have been allowed to use the building for a special occasion.

Tullahoma is a special place in south Tennessee where Coca-Cola memories are treasured, saved, and being made every day!

Chapter 5
Signs Across Georgia

A University of Georgia art professor once told a newspaper reporter "if you are in the restoration business, you are not in business until you have restored a Coca-Cola sign, and we have done about twelve of them."

Professor Joseph Norman of the university's Lamar Dodd School of Art had worked with his students to form a group called "Color The World Bright" and in 2012 they began to restore and create signs throughout the state.

The old murals often become community landmarks and funds to have them restored is often raised by local organizations, businesses or even concerned individuals. The student group is contacted and the participating artists are paid for their work which can include researching details of the original sign, surface repair and preparation, as well as the actual painting. Professor Newman

Photo courtesy of Lake Oconee Living Magazine

explained the students will earn from $200 to $1,000 each along with valuable experience and "bragging rights."

A project in the spring of 2019 required the students to restore multiple Coca-Cola ghost signs on a large building in Conyers. Built in 1925 the building first served as a furniture warehouse, then a railroad mill, next an antique store and finally as the Point Olde Town Tavern. The Conyers-Rockdale Council for the Arts worked in partnership with the city of Conyers to make the large restoration project possible. Coca-Cola signs had to be restored on three sides of the building along with a sign for the furniture company which first occupied the structure.

Mayor Vince Evans said "the restoration project demonstrates that

Conyers supports the arts and the story it tells of our past." He added that the landmark building in Olde Town Conyers "had been brought back to life in a vibrant way."

The art students restored another large Coca-Cola mural which filled almost the entire side of a three story building in Elberton. The badly faded sign was located downtown on the rear of the Stan's Music World building. It had become difficult to even read the phrase "Relieves Fatigue," a slogan used by Coca-Cola from 1907 to 1911.

The city of Elberton provided the funds to restore the sign. City Manager Lanier Dunn explained that Coca-Cola murals are very popular in the south, and the restored sign provides an attraction for local citizens as well as visitors and tourists.

In the early 1900s many beverage bottlers saw the growing popularity of Coca-Cola and dozens of "knock-off" drinks were created. One of the best known of the renegade beverages was Chero-Cola which was operating plants in several southern communities, including one built in 1913 in Greensboro, Georgia.

The "Color the World Bright" students preserved the memory of that drink when they restored Chero-Cola murals on two buildings which had housed the bottling operation. The first site in Greensboro was a building which Chero-Cola occupied for only a year. Later it became a cotton mill and finally in 2019 when the mural was restored, it had become a brew pub called Oconee Brewing Company.

At one time there actually were two murals on the brewing company building. The first was located on a rear wall which collapsed during

building renovations. The second sign, the one restored, was located on a side wall facing the parking lot.

The reason for the original creation of the second sign became a mystery as research revealed the sign had been first painted after 1941. But Chero-Cola had gone out of business years earlier after loosing a lawsuit where Coca-Cola successfully claimed ownership of the word "cola".

A court reversed that decision in 1942 but it was too late for Chero-Cola to make a come back. Some believe the sign which was painted in the 40's may simply have been a nostalgic shot at Coca-Cola because the mural included the words "the winning drink." In a program to honor Greensboro's history, the restoration was sponsored by Coldwell Banker Lake Oconee Realty.

Chero-Cola moved its operation in 1914 from Greensboro to Madison, about 17 miles west, and installed $6,000 worth of new bottling equipment in a building owned by J.B. Sword, who was a distiller of whiskey and also operated a saloon. However, Georgia prohibition in 1915 created the

opportunity for a soft drink company to operate in the building.

The students complete the mural restoration on the side of the Sword building in September 2019, almost a century after Chero-Cola had been forced out of business. The restoration was sponsored by the Morgan County Landmarks Organization which earned a "Preservation Intervention" award for saving an important historic landmark. The structure in 2020 served as the Madison Public Safety building.

A second Greensboro mural was done in 2019 to observe the 50th anniversary of the popular Coca-Cola slogan "It's the Real Thing". The city of Greensboro sponsored the students for that project.

Non-Coca-Cola examples of the art student's outdoor talent are being enjoyed at numerous locations throughout the state. Included are a large city mural in Tignall, several church murals in Athens, a railroad sign in Union Point, numerous University of Georgia related murals, and a colorful original mural created by the students which welcomes visitors to the Uncle Remus Museum in Eatonton.

One of the oldest remaining Coca-Cola plants in the nation received a mural restoration by the Georgia art students in 2020 as the building was being prepared for a new life. Built in 1903 in Columbus, Georgia the plant was only the third to be licensed in Coca-Cola's home state.

The bottling franchise for the area was obtained in 1901 by an Alabama businessman, Columbus Roberts Sr. who was a successful grocer in Opelika and had noticed the increasing number of customers buying Coca-Cola. Roberts convinced his brother-in-law, George S. Cobb, Sr. to join him in the new bottling venture in Georgia. However Cobb stayed only a short time at the Columbus plant, moving on to establish plants in LaGrange and West Point, Georgia.

Bottling continued at the Columbus plant until 1940. After that

the large brick structure had a number of uses until being purchased as a storage facility by technology giant TSYS. Local attorney Ken Henson Jr. purchased the building from TSYS in 2019 and applied for city rezoning to allow both apartments and office use.

While remodeling the interior of his new purchase Henson also contacted the university art students to have them restore the Coca-Cola identification to the side of the building. During the plant's bottling days Coca-Cola signage occupied the entire front of the building.

Eight months of research and planning with the owner were needed before the students could spend a weekend bringing the 100-year-old sign back to life. Henson had emphasized the old building's historic value to the city.

However, it also is important to note Columbus's even older and other significant place in early Coca-Cola history. Columbus claims to be the "birthplace" of Coca-Cola because John Pemberton, the pharmacist who created the original Coca-Cola syrup was living and working in Columbus

at the time. Local historians believe Pemberton developed his secret formula while working at Eagle Drug and Chemical Company in Columbus.

Pemberton had moved to Columbus in 1853, and the house where he lived is now owned by the Historic Columbus Foundation; his apothecary shop has been recreated at the site. Coca-Cola mementos, pharmaceutical items, a soda fountain and old advertisements also are on display.

Pemberton died in 1888 and his grave can be viewed in the city's Linwood Cemetery.

Through the years Atlanta also has claimed the Coca-Cola syrup was created there after Pemberton had relocated to the city. Both Columbus and Atlanta have each established a historical marker with that designation. However, retired Coca-Cola archivist, Phil Mooney has taken a position in favor of Columbus saying the syrup was created there and taken later to Atlanta by Pemberton.

Chapter 6
Scottsboro Old Soda Fountain

It is said to be the oldest business in Alabama, and also it was one of the first in the state to sell Coca-Cola. In addition, the interesting history of the old business includes a direct family connection to the very first days of Coca-Cola bottling.

Now known as Payne's Soda Fountain and Sandwich Shop, the business began in 1869 as W. H. Payne Drug Company of Scottsboro, Alabama. It actually began operating one year before the town of Scottsboro officially incorporated.

Druggist William Henry Payne opened the store after returning from the civil war. At first his business was located near the railroad, on the northwest side of the community square, where most of the early town had been built. Payne was a compounding pharmacist and created remedies such as syrup of wild cherry and Eureka itch and tetter ointment.

He also sold cold sparkling soda water, believed to have medicinal powers, for 5-cents per glass.

Five years later the Jackson County courthouse was built and Payne moved his drug store to a two story brick building he had constructed on the courthouse square where the business remained for over one and one-half centuries.

Payne died in 1899, and his son James Robinson Payne operated the business until his death in the 1940s. The historic building has remained under the ownership of James Payne's daughter, Elizabeth Payne Word. But the business has been operated through the years by non-Payne family owners.

The building's connection to the very first days of Coca-Cola bottling is because of Elizabeth's family history. Her great uncle was George Hunter of Chattanooga. Hunter had become the owner of the Coca-Cola "parent" bottling enterprise, originally created and developed by his uncle Ben Thomas. Thomas and his partner Joseph Whitehead obtained in 1899 exclusive U.S. rights for the bottling of Coca-Cola. The rapid growth of Coca-Cola then began when they, acting as "parent" bottlers, started selling territory rights to other bottlers.

As Thomas aged, and having no children, he had selected Hunter to take over the management and ultimately

Construction of Payne's Drug Store

inherit his growing Coca-Cola business. Hunter became a strong supporter of the individual bottlers, and is recognized for his successful legal battle with Coca-Cola to save the bottlers' lifetime contracts.

Meanwhile growth continued at the drug store. A 20-foot long soda fountain was added in 1939, and quickly became a popular attraction with new soda jerks being hired to serve the grow-ing number of customers. The first step for food service also began, as Payne's started selling hot dogs topped with a now

Payne's Drug Store interior

famous red slaw, said to have been created from a secret old family recipe.

Curbside service was provided at Payne's in the 1940s and '50s with Coca-Cola and ice cream delivered by the soda jerks to parked customers outside.

The pharmacy portion of the business was closed in 1991, but the popular soda fountain and sandwich shop has continued through the years. The business ownership and management changed again in 2013, when mother and daughter Lisa Garrett and Jessica Walton took over.

Previously Garrett had created a '50s type dinning area in her home in Bridgeport, Tennessee and also operated a luncheon in Sewanee, Ten-nessee, and she was looking for a new opportunity when Payne's became available. Memorabilia items from her home, including a jukebox and advertising signs were used to create the new atmosphere at Payne's. Also added were red vinyl chairs, a checker board floor and chrome bar stools. The red slaw hot dog still tops the menu, but a variety of other sandwich-es have been added, including a Dagwood and a Reuben. There also is a selection of salads and daily menu specials.

Payne's Drug Store owners, Lisa Garrett and Jessica Walton

The old 20-foot soda fountain sustained a mechanical problem, and temporarily was being used only to serve ice cream, while a search was underway to locate a fountain repairman. A special logo sign was created in 2019 to honor Payne's 150 years of making memories in Scottsboro.

Jessica said, "everyone has a story about Payne's, but if they don't we'll help them make one." Jessica and Lisa said they are proud to be running a business with such a long and important history in Alabama.

Coca-Cola was first bottled in Scottsboro in 1912 and the franchise went through several

ownership changes before being acquired in 2014 by the nation's third largest bottler, Coca-Cola United of Birmingham.

Business partners Charley Beard and A.B. Brandon started the bottling business, but in 1918 Beard bought out his partner and continued to bottle and sell Coca-Cola for eight years.

The next owner, Walter Daniel built a two-story brick building for his Coca-Cola plant. When Daniel died in 1938, his widow and the plant manager Tom Sisk continued the business for another five years before selling to Joseph L. Bean of Chattanooga.

Hamlin Caldwell, who became known as "Mr. Coca-Cola in Scottsboro" became plant manager in 1955, and remained in that position for nearly thirty-five years. He oversaw a

1957 addition which doubled the plant's floor space, and 23-years later he was there when a new 40,000 sq. ft. facility was opened to serve northeast Alabama and part of Georgia. That new building construction followed the merger of the Fort Payne Coca-Cola business to Scottsboro.

The business at that time was owned by Johnston Coca-Cola Bottling of Chattanooga, and the actual bottling had been moved to a company plant in Cleveland, Tennessee while the Scottsboro facility provided area distribution. Johnston bottling merged with Coca-Cola corporate on 1991.

In 2020 Coca-Cola United continued the Scottsboro tradition with their facility on John T. Reid Parkway.

Chapter 7
Decatur Museum

A Coca-Cola museum filled with rare "treasures" and located in a former railway depot, is the achievement of an avid collector who's interest in Coca-Cola was piqued over thirty years earlier by a simple Coca-Cola poster.

As his interest evolved David Lee ultimately became a frequent visitor and buyer at collector shows, flea markets and private sales searching for rare discoveries to place in his ever expanding museum near Decatur, Illinois.

It started in 1989 when David was working in a gift store and a poster print of a crushed Coca-Cola can captured his interest and served to start his search for old Coca-Cola bottles and other smaller memorabilia items. The clever Coca-Cola commercials at that time also added to David's decision that Coca-Cola would be "a cool collectible".

His collection expanded into a new dimension with the first purchase of an

David Lee

old vending machine. Within nine years, and conveniently living alone, he managed to fill his home with Coca-Cola memorabilia. Income to support his ever growing "Coke addiction" was provided by the previous purchase of a local disc jockey music business which had become a popular success.

David opened his first museum in the summer of 2008 when he took ten vending machines, a variety of old signs, bottles and other items to a leased space in a nearby shopping mall.

Unfortunately, like many small shopping malls at that time, customer traffic continued to decline, and after three years David closed the display and put his museum back into storage.

Still determined to display his Coca-Cola collection, in 2013 David purchased a semi trailer truck which would hold about one-fourth of his collection. For the next three years the scaled down Coca-Cola museum hit the road, as David was hired to bring his unique display to festivals and other public events.

A 2017 marriage apparently was the catalyst which triggered

a search for a new home for David and his wife and for a permanent location for the Coca-Cola museum. The search ended during a visit to a nearby antique mall, where instead of buying antiques, David decided to purchase the entire building, a former interurban railway depot in Harristown.

The result of that purchase was a major renovation project to create a modern home for the couple as well an adjacent exhibit area for the still growing Coca-Cola collection.

The building remodeling had progressed well enough by the summer of 2019 that scheduled museum tours were being provided, with regular public viewing hours to be announced.

One of the first groups to visit was a Coca-Cola collectors club from St. Louis.

At last count the museum had over 30 old vending machines on

Photo courtesy of Gateway to the West Collectors Chapter

display, including a rare double sided Cavalier 102. The unit is one of only 500 manufactured in the 1950's, and it is believed less than one-hundred still exist.

Another rare attraction is a 1976 Ford Coca-Cola – Levi Strauss custom van. Only 15 of the unique vehicles were built by the Goodies Company of Illinois for a special joint promotion by Coca-Cola and Levi Strauss. The van was designed by "Hot Rod" magazine and included a TV, refrigerator, and denim and shag carpet interior. During his search for the Levi van David had actually purchased three of the units, keeping the best one for his museum and selling the other two.

Four very rare "Cobots" are featured in another interesting display. The name "Cobot" was created by combining the words Coke and Robot, for a remote controlled robot designed by Coca-Cola in the 1970s. The unit was made to resemble "R2-D2" from the popular Star Wars movie. However it has been reported that close similarity may have caused Coca-Cola to stop the manufacturing of the Cobot. Consequently the remaining robots are among the rarest items in the search for Coca-Cola collectibles.

The body of the Cobot looks like a soda can, while the feet are each made of three miniature Coca-Cola bottles. Special graphics kits were

Photo courtesy of Gateway to the West Collectors Chapter

available to bottlers, so they could change the body appearance from a Coca-Cola can to a Sprite can or other Coca-Cola product. The museum also has samples of those rare logo change kits.

A large neon Coca-Cola fish tail sign stands out among the more than 50 old signs on display. The classic neon, which was obtained from an old area grocery store, is 6 ½ feet wide by 2 ½ feet high.

The museum also has what may be

the largest display of "can art," which are items fashioned from Coca-Cola cans. A highlight of the display is a six piece can art train set which was given to the museum. Included in the train is a box car with the door opened to reveal a load of tiny Coca-Cola cases.

On display are more than 25 one-of-a-kind can creations, including ships, cars, planes, a wind chime and a lamp. Visitors to the museum are reminded of how it all got started by the framed crushed can poster proudly displayed at the entrance. Coca-Cola bottling began in Decatur in 1903, making it the second city in Illinois to have a Coca-Cola plant; the first was Chicago two years earlier. The initial plant remained at a location on South Franklin for over two decades until owners J. M. Scherer and C. P. Housman decided to build a larger plant on East Cantrell. The business was purchased in 1948 by W. R. Hayes and his two sons from DuQuoin. They initiated a major plant renovation which allowed production to increase to 280 bottles per minute. Merle Carroll became president of Decatur Bottling in 1958 and the plant moved to a building at 300 E. Eldorado, which previously housed a Chevrolet dealership. Decatur Coca-Cola had become part of a seventeen plant bottling business operating in Illinois, Missouri and Kentucky, which was owned by W. B Terry of Lexington. Bottling production at Decatur was halted in 1967 and plans for a new warehouse facility on the east side of town were announced in 1970.

Terry also owned restaurants and hotels, and was a real estate developer. The Decatur school district purchased the former plant building and Coca-Cola distributing was moved in 1971 to a new location at 3220 N. Woodford St.

The seventeen plant Coca-Cola bottling business was later acquired by Coca-Cola corporate's CCE division, and Decatur distribution was merged with the Springfield facility. But in 2017 the bottling group became Heartland Coca-Cola, when it was sold to former pro basketball star Junior Bridgeman, who had a twelve year career with the Milwaukee Bucks.

Chapter 8
Dothan, Alabama

An abandoned Coca-Cola bottling plant in Dothan, Alabama has been brought back to life with music and song.

It all began in the spring of 2017 when a local businessman, with a family history in Dothan, realized his hometown needed an entertainment venue. Alan Clark owns a security

business which often provides the on site protection for concerts and other events. He and his family were returning from a concert in Panama City, Florida when their conversation turned to the idea of having live entertainment in Dothan.

Alan explained his thoughts, saying as he drove, "we need to do this, to offer a new entertainment source for Dothan, especially for young adults." Clark's son Boyd believed entertainment to be an important part of a community's quality of life, and his daughter Mary urged the location of an entertainment facility should be in the city's downtown.

It was that idea which reminded Clark of the former Coca-Cola bottling plant, a 48,000 sq. ft. building which had sat empty for twenty years. It is located on a four- acre site, which once was considered the location for a proposed minor league baseball team.

Clark's idea quickly moved forward, and in just of couple days he had located and talked with the plant's owner. An investment company in Cartersville, Georgia originally had acquired six abandoned Coca-Cola plants, and the Dothan facility was one of two remaining for sale.

However, the owner explained an offer to purchase Dothan by another individual, was already being considered. Clark moved fast with his proposal, and within three weeks he became the owner of the four acre site which included the large abandoned plant, which he had not yet even seen from the inside. He said he was more interested in having the adjacent land become the site for an outdoor amphitheater.

It might have been the intriguing lure of the old plant which lead to the decision to immediately include a portion of the building in the plans. Work moved quickly in the former shops area, and despite unanticipated problems, in just six months a concert facility was ready to accommodate 1800 people. The inaugural event, held in December, featured a popular musical group from Austin, Texas.

A large professional stage had been constructed, along with adjacent customer service facilities which included a full service restaurant, a bar area, and modern restrooms. The old wood from the former truck shops

was salvaged and used in construction of the new bar area. Other salvaged plant pieces were utilized throughout the restoration, and in the process a variety of Coca-Cola memories were uncovered, including old signs, bottles and vending equipment.

The new entertainment facility, now simply known as "The Plant", has proven to be a success in creating a popular attraction for downtown Dothan. What followed next for the Clark family was the restoration and repurposing of the remainder of a very large old building. Another type of restaurant, boutique shops, even offices may find a home in this important part of Coca-Cola history, which needed to be preserved.

Coca-Cola was first bottled in Dothan in 1906 in a small plant at East Adams and North St. Andrews, a permanent location which was expanded several times during the bottling days , and where "The Plant" remains today.

Alan Clark leads a tour and discusses his plans for the old Coca-Cola plant. With him are daughters of former plant owner and bottling pioneer, Stanhope Elmore, Jr. Katie Wolverton of Panama Beach and Jane Elmore of Birmingham, raised in Dothan, share memories of those Coca-Cola days.

Left to right: Henry Crine, Bookkeeper; G.M. Lewis Sr., Manager/Partner; Ottis Meadows, Mechanic; H.H. Head, plant foreman; James Phillips, Assistant Foreman.

The history of that plant is unique, as included are the names of two Alabama families remembered for their achievements in the very early days of Coca-Cola bottling, as well as their contributions to the history of the state of Alabama. It's the stories of the Elmores and the Bellingraths.

The Bellingrath brothers, Walter and William, began their journey into Coca-Cola history in 1903 with the purchase of territory and the start of bottling in Montgomery and then Mobile. Their belief in the business of Coca-Cola bottling continued as they went on to establish several more locations, including the plant in Dothan.

The Elmore family is deeply rooted in American history. John Archer Elmore, at the age of fourteen, fought for his country's freedom in the Revolutionary War. He was born in Virginia but began the family's

Alabama legacy when he moved to Autanga in 1819.

When a new Alabama county was created in 1866 it was named Elmore County to honor General John Archer Elmore.

John's son, Albert Stanhope Elmore became the first native Alabamian to serve as secretary of state. A daughter, Sarah Elmore, became the wife of Governor Benjamin Fitzpatrick. Another son, Physic Rush Elmore was appointed a federal judge in Independence, Kansas.

The judge's son, Nesbitt Elmore had two children, Stanhope Elmore and Mary Nesbitt Elmore, who ultimately would begin the family's Coca-Cola adventure.

Nesbitt wanted his children to be educated in Alabama, and Mary moved to Montgomery in the early 1900s. In 1906 she met and married William Bellingrath, who had become a Coca-Cola bottler with his brother Walter just three years earlier.

Mary's brother Stanhope moved to Montgomery as a student in 1910, where he also began working part time in the Coca-Cola plant. William took a liking to Stanhope, which fueled the young man's interest in the Coca-Cola bottling business. When William died in 1938, Stanhope was able to help his sister manage and operate the Montgomery plant.

Stanhope Elemore, Sr. Photo courtesy of University of Alabama Department of Archives and History

Soon after beginning bottling in Montgomery, the Bellingraths acquired the rights for Mobile, and Walter moved to establish that new location. The Bellingraths continued to acquire additional Coca-Cola territories, often establishing partnerships with other family members.

A Bellingrath sister, Mamie and her husband John Burnett had the plant in Andalusia, Alabama. Another sister, Kate and her husband W. N. Brown were operating the Selma plant. Brother Theodore Leon had the facility in Little Rock, Arkansas and another brother, Leonard Ferdinand was bottling Coca-Cola in Pine Bluff, Arkansas.

However, in Dothan ownership initially did not include another family member. William selected a Mobile Coca-Cola salesman, Marvin Lewis to become the managing partner, and Lewis received a 25-percent share of the business.

A legal business notice in the Dothan Eagle newspaper in 1909 was signed by W. A. Bellingrath and G. M. Lewis. The notice described the wording on the bottle with Coca-Cola identification as "Bellingrath" and "Property of W. A. B. Coca-Cola Bottling Co. of Dothan, Ala." On the bottom of the bottles were the letters "W.A.B.". The wording on the bottle cases was similar along with the additional messages: "drink Coca-Cola 5c" and "when empty return to Coca-Cola Bottling Company, Dothan, Ala.

Those early bottling days were a challenge for Marvin Lewis as he reported the grape, orange and other flavors of soda were outselling Coca-Cola. To help promote the new beverage, he began adding a few bottles of Coca-Cola to the cases of flavored drinks. This was a common marketing tactic for many bottlers in those early days.

Photo courtesy of Frank Gaines Photography

However, growth came quickly and an article in 1923 in the Dothan Eagle reported "One of Dothan's most valued industries and one that takes its place as a leader in its field in all of Alabama is the Dothan Coca-Cola Bottling Company." It further noted that the company's motor trucks daily supplied some 500 dealers in its territory. It referred to Coca-Cola as "the world's greatest drink".

For fifty years the price of 80-cents was charged for a case of twenty-four 6.5 ounce bottles of Coca-Cola. Finally in 1956 the case price was increased to 96-cents. A 10 ounce bottle was introduced in 1960. In 1962 Sprite was introduced, along with other Coca-Cola brands including Fanta, Fresca, Tab, Mr. Pibb, and Mellow-Yellow. The plant discontinued its private line of flavored drinks.

Lewis' son, Marvin Jr. started working at the Dothan plant during the summers, while attending school in Chattanooga 1931-1935. He became employed full time as advertising director in 1935. His father died in 1946.

Meanwhile in Montgomery the Stanhope Elmore family had been growing with the birth of five children, including Stanhope Jr. who would grow to play an important role in the Dothan plant.

In 1947 young Stanhope Elmore became manager and partner in a plant his father had acquired in Independence, Kansas. Five years later his father urged him to move to Dothan, again to assume a management and ownership role. Consequently Dothan became the home

Coca-Cola promotional event in Dothan. Stanhope Elmore, Jr. on the left, his father Stanhope, Sr. second from the right.

for the Stanhope Elmore Jr. family for the next five decades. He managed the plant until retirement in 1986, and during the early years received advise and assistance from his father who remained in Montgomery.

Stanhope Elmore Sr. died in 1961. An article in the "Coca-Cola Bottler" magazine recognized his contribution to the business, listing his career as "manager of Coca-Cola Companies in Dothan, Montgomery, Tuscaloosa, Troy, and Andalusia."

The Andalusia plant was closed and merged with Dothan in 1980. During the 75th anniversary celebration of the Dothan plant in 1981, Elmore's prediction for the the future was "Coca-Cola would outsell coffee, tea and milk, and each person in the Dothan area would enjoy Coca-Cola about 700 times per year."

Bottling was stopped at the Dothan plant in the early 1980's, with Coca-Cola products being received from Montgomery. Dothan, Montgomery, Tuscaloosa, and several other plants were sold by Elmore-Belingrath LLC in 1998 to Coca-Cola (CCE). Walter Bellingrath's plant in

Photo courtesy of Frank Gaines Photography

Mobile had been sold earlier in 1981 by the Bellingrath Foundation to a large bottler from Miami. Stanhope Elmore, Jr. died in Dothan in 2002.

Coca-Cola continued to operate at the downtown Dothan location for about two years, until moving to a new location on the city's northwest side.

Dothan Coca-Cola changed ownership one more time when it was acquired in 2013 by Coca-Cola United of Birmingham.

Chapter 9
Andalusia, Alabama

A "sister plant" to Dothan, Coca-Cola of Andalusia was also planned to become a community entertainment attraction by 2021. Located only 75 miles west of Dothan in southern Alabama, the Andalusia business began as another Bellingrath Coca-Cola plant. Bottling began in 1906 with the franchise being owned by "Mamie" Bellingrath Burnett, sister of William and Walter Bellingrath who established Coca-Cola businesses in several Alabama cities.

The last Bellingrath plant facility to be constructed in Andalusia was built in 1950, but had sat empty for over twenty years when Kyle and Kim Baumgartner presented the city their idea for an exciting new use for the

old plant. The city had purchased the building and land six years earlier with the goal of "preserving another piece of the city's history."

The Baumgartners had worked with New Orleans architects to create a restoration plan which would embrace the nostalgia of the former Coca-Cola landmark. City officials learned details of a planned family friendly venue with both indoor and outdoor entertainment areas. Inside included an up-scale

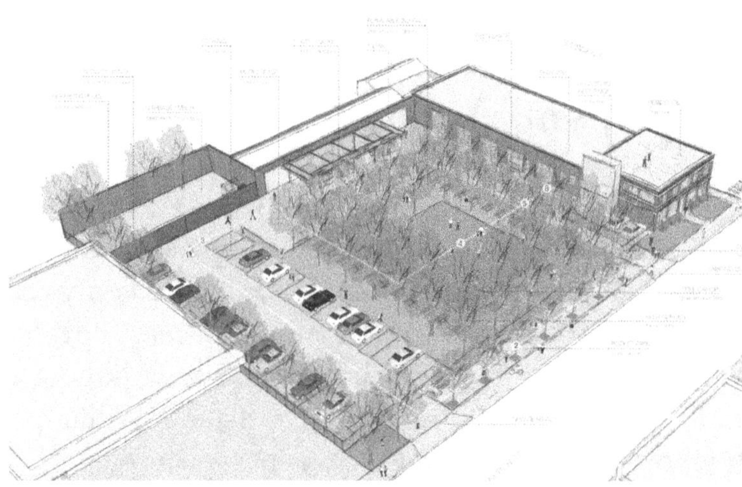

restaurant and pub called "The B" which featured a specialty menu along with wine and beer service. Another area included space for live entertainment and large screen televisions for viewing sports and other special events. Outside activities offered were shuffleboard, ping-pong, sidewalk chalk art and food trucks. The 12,000 sq. ft. structure is located on a one acre site.

The city agreed to sell the building and land to the Baumgartners for $140,000 and that future taxes generated by the business would be used in part to repay the city's initial investment in site improvements. The new attraction became part of Andalusia's downtown entertainment district and compliments other business attractions which are also located in the area.

Coca-Cola was first bottled in Andalusia in a small rented building where bottling was done by hand and the Coca-Cola was delivered by horse and wagon. Rail was used to ship bottles to outlying locations. The business grew quickly under the management of Mamie's husband John Burnett, and by 1914 it was necessary to relocate to a larger building; motor trucks were used for the first time to make deliveries.

A second business The Consumer Ice and Cold Storage Company was established by Burnett in 1923. When John died in 1928 his nephew,

George Ether-
idge became
manager, and
two years later
moved to a
new bottling
facility de-
scribed at that
time as "one
of the most

modern" in the state.

The plant included modern bottling equipment which could fill 150 bottles per minute and produce more than 25 different types of packages. A fleet of 16 trucks were required to serve the increasing number of area customers. The ice business was positioned adjacent to the new plant, and some employees would work in both facilities.

Etheridge died suddenly in 1937 and Mrs. Burnett died the following year with the business becoming part of the Bellingrath estate, and John Hilson being transferred from Montgomery to manage the Andalusia operation.

By 1950 another new production facility was needed, and what became the last Bellingrath plant in Andalusia was built at a cost of $140,000. The opening was celebrated by the community with a ceremony and open house event April 26, 1950.

The last Coca-Cola to be bottled in Andalusia was on January 18, 1980 with the plant being closed later that year and merged with the Bellingrath plant in Dothan. The downtown Dothan Coca-Cola plant was sold and closed in 2004. Dothan became part of Coca-Cola United of Birmingham in 2013.

However the old Dothan and Andalusia plants are "sisters" again providing entertainment as part of a growing national trend to restore and find new lives for historic buildings.

Chapter 10
Ottawa, Kansas

Almost everyone has a special high school memory which includes Coca-Cola, whether at a favorite soda fountain, football game or high school dance.

What could be a better place for a high school class reunion than an old Coca-Cola bottling plant? The former Coca-Cola plant in Ottawa, Kansas is available. Now restored

as an event center known as "The Bottle House", it has become a popular place for class reunions, weddings, and a variety of other social and business activities.

John Going (left) meeting with two "Bottle Shop" owners, Jason Maxwell and William Crowley, to discuss plans for John's class reunion.

For John Going, a member of the Ottawa class of 1959, his class reunion at The Bottle House contained more than high school days memories. John's father, Jack Going was an owner and the manager when the Coca-Cola plant was built in 1940.

Jack and his partner Stanhope Elmore Sr.

A very young John Going shows off his new uniform

had purchased Ottawa's Coca-Cola business in 1939, and immediately announced plans for the new building. Elmore was an early Coca-Cola bottling pioneer, having previously established several plants in Alabama and Kansas. He also was Jack Going's uncle, as Jack's father had married Stanhope's sister, Jeanette Elmore.

After bottling was stopped in Ottawa in 1963, the building had several uses before finally becoming an event center. It was sold to become a farmers supply store in 1965. Later it became a soda shop and an antique mall for twenty years until being closed again, and then offered for sale in January 2015.

Eighteen months later the building was acquired by a group of six area investors, and Melinda Heyn became manager. Building renovations began quickly with the work being monitored by the Franklin County Historical Society, to maintain the integrity of the city's historical district.

The building's interior retained a rustic style, and a metal storefront on the east side was removed to reveal the plant's original exterior appearance. The "Bottle House" opened for its first event in September 2017, just a year after the start of the restoration. Work then began to obtain historical registration for the structure.

Coca-Cola bottling actually came to Ottawa in 1912, although it had been advertised as a soda fountain drink as early as 1899. However, the bottling of flavored sodas began even earlier, when E. T. Snyder started the bottling business in 1885. Snyder's first drinks were ginger ale, champaign cider and a beverage called birch beer.

Snyder's business was purchased in 1896 by Ike M. Reed, and it became Ottawa Bottling Works in 1899, with root beer, a new flavor added to the soda choices. Two years later Reed boasted the plant could produce

300 cases per day because of a recent purchase of two new bottling machines.

Reed sold one-half interest in Ottawa Bottling to B. D. Bennett in 1904, and plans for a new 40' x 60' building were announced. The business had been operating in shared space in the Forest Park Creamery. About a year later Ottawa

Bottling advertised it could produce a total of twenty soda flavors.

Howard McGee, who had been a telegraph operator for the Santa Fe Railroad, accepted a position at Ottawa Bottling in 1910, and two years later McGee purchased Reed's remaining half interest in the business. McGee went on to also acquire the Garnett Bottling Works in Garnett in 1913, but

Jack Going

died that same year after a brief illness. He was 27 years old.

Bennett and his two sons continued to operate Ottawa bottling, and by 1921 had increased production capabilities to 500 cases per day.

Jack Going and Stanhope Elmore purchased the business in 1939. At that time Going was sales manager for the Kansas City Coca-Cola Company, working from Excelsior Springs. Going relocated to Ottawa to manage their new venture, while Elmore continued his Coca-Cola activities from Montgomery, Alabama.

They quickly announced plans for a new plant to be constructed at the site of the old "Ottawa House, which for many years had been a well known area hotel. Additional business and residential property adjacent to the hotel site also had to be acquired with the cost of the new plant estimated to be at least $30,000.

During the following years of operation, Ottawa Coca-Cola was instrumental in introducing new products and bottling innovations, often receiving special recognition from the Coca-Cola Company.

Jack Going died in 1954, and his widow Jane Going took over the business until it was sold in 1960 to R.C. Winchester, who was an officer with the Ottawa Steel Company. The Ottawa plant again received national recognition when in 1961 it was the first U.S. distributor to introduce Coca-Cola's new line of Fanta beverages.

When Jack Going first became involved in Ottawa Coca-Cola he was working at that time with Kansas City Coca-Cola bottling. Ironically the Ottawa plant and territory became part of the Kansas City operation when it was sold by Winchester in January 1963. The president of Kansas City Coca-Cola announced the bottling line in Ottawa would be shut down with the building to become a distribution facility.

However, the use as a warehouse was discontinued just two years later. Then what followed was 50-years of changes for the historic building until it finally became "The Bottle House", a new place of community pride and enjoyment in Ottawa, Kansas.

Chapter 11
Quincy Millionaires

Many stories have been told about how investing in Coca-Cola in the early years created millionaires in a small town in north Florida. At one time it was reported there were more millionaires per capita in Quincy, Florida than any other place in America, and it was credited to investments made in Coca-Cola during years of phenomenal company growth.

But where did the "start up" money come from to make possible those early stock purchases, and what created the initial Coca-Cola connection? That history includes two natural products, at one time exclusive to the Quincy area, and a business relationship between a local banker and a Coca-Cola corporate president.

Years before Coca-Cola was invented Quincy already was experiencing financial growth because of tobacco and as a result of a special type of soil accidentally discovered in the area. The tobacco product called Shade tobacco was brought to Quincy for cultivation in 1880 by John Smith, an experienced farmer from Virginia. Shade tobacco produces a leaf which is used in the wrapping of cigars. It grew

exceptionally well in the region's humid climate and eventually become Gadsden county's most profitable industry. Quincy became known as the "Shade-grown leaf tobacco capital," and that tobacco was grown only in one other location in Connecticut.

The Owl Commercial Company was one of the largest of the many tobacco companies which located in Quincy. The company produced the White Owl and Robert Burns lines of cigars. It operated with a labor force of over 500 men, many who were immigrants from Germany and would discover another source of prosperity for Quincy. While digging a company well they recognized a gray clay material which they had seen in their home country.

Known as "Fullers Earth" the unique soil is used as an absorbent for oil, grease, and animal waste. Also used in early auto oil filters, cat litter, and as a carrier for pesticides and fertilizer. The 1893 discovery in Quincy was the first location

for the substance in the country. Previously it all had been imported from England. By 1939 the mines at Quincy were providing half of the nation's production, and by 2005 the U.S. had become the world's largest producer with almost 70-percent of the market. Since first discovered in Quincy, Fullers Earth has been mined in 24 states.

What ultimately lead to the community's Coca-Cola wealth occurred when a prominent Quincy businessman, Mark Welch "Pat" Munroe saw the need for a local bank to facilitate the growing financial needs of the community. Pat, his brother and his mother were on the bank's board and Pat became president when the Quincy State Bank was formed in 1892. He served in that position until he died in 1940, and during those fifty years made many bank investments and business connections.

One of those bank investments was with a large diversified company in Columbus, Georgia which was owned by W. C. Bradley, who later became a president

Quincy State Bank

of the Coca-Cola Corporation. Munroe had been watching the growth of Coca-Cola and commented that even during hard times people would spend their last nickels to buy bottles of Coca-Cola.

In 1919 over $1 million was deposited in the Quincy State Bank, and that same year Coca-Cola stock went public after the company was purchased by a syndicate headed by Ernest Woodruff, who also was from Columbus and was W. C. Bradley's neighbor. Bradley became one of the largest individual investors in Coca-Cola and was named president of the company's financial and legal affairs when Woodruff's group took over.

Seeking to expand Coca-Cola's operation, Bradley contacted his old business friend Pat Munroe in Quincy and convinced him to invest, which he did in 1920, purchasing numerous Coca-Cola shares for the bank and for himself. Munroe then strongly encouraged bank customers and friends to do the same.

Folklore described Munroe as a "Coke Evangelist" and it was said if you went to "borrow a quarter at his bank you would be persuaded to buy a nickel's worth" of Coca-Cola stock.

The son of a state representative at that time told how his father went to the bank for a $2000 loan and Munroe gave him $4000 if he agreed to purchase $2000 in Coca-Cola stock. Another son of a former bank customer recalled how his father refused an offer to purchase $5000 in stock in the 1920s. He explained with regret that stock would have been worth $500,000 by 1975.

Pat Munroe (right) with Coca-Cola investor E.B. Shefler, a local Shade tobacco producer.

The Quincy State Bank

did not fail and remained open during the economic crisis of the great depression thanks to continued Coca-Cola dividends and support from the town's Coca-Cola millionaires. Pat Munroe often said "never sell Coca-Cola stock."

The Quincy State Bank was acquired in 2004 by Capital City Bank of Tallahassee. But the impact of the Coca-Cola millionaires remains visible throughout the city. Stately mansions, some still owned by families of the original Coca-Cola investors, can be admired as part of the city's popular walking tour.

A guide brochure which explains the tour is available at the Quincy Main Street office, 104 N. Adams Street. The office also has a display of local Coca-Cola memorabilia on loan from Joe Munroe, grandson of Pat Munroe the popular Coca-Cola banker. The display includes a damaged vending machine which came from the area's most raucous and infamous honky tonk, the Shady Rest, which was located between Quincy and Havana. A testament to the previous use is a large bullet hole in the machine's side.

A classic style Coca-Cola mural is often photographed by visitors at the Padgett Jewelry store at 21 E. Jefferson St. The sign was painted in the 1960's by Coca-Cola, and several corporate officials were present for the unveiling. Among them was Vice Chairman Roberto Goizueta who

later would be CEO during the ill-fated "New Coca-Cola" controversy.

The restoration of an historic theater was possible because of donations from heirs of Coca-Cola millionaires. The "Leaf Theater" was built in 1949 and named because of the importance of Shade tobacco in the

community. The grand opening was hosted by Roy Rogers, but the theater was forced to close in 1980 due to competition from the new multi theaters. Pat Munroe's daughter, Julia Woodward was one of the heirs who helped with the restoration in 1983 when the building was then donated to the Quincy Music Theater group.

Coca-Cola also was bottled in Quincy when the Middleton family opened a plant in 1909. The business was sold to Coca-Cola in the 1980's and the plant was closed; the business merged with Coca-Cola bottling in Bainbridge, Georgia about 25 miles away. The Bainbridge operation was acquired in 2017 by Coca-Cola United of Birmingham. The facility was closed two years later and consolidated with other area plants including Tallahassee.

Quincy has become a quiet rural town with a population of less than 7,000 people. It long ago lost its claim as the richest small town in America as original Coca-Cola investors have died, and many heirs have moved away. In fact Gadsden county ranks as one of the lowest per-capita income counties in Florida. But it's also reported that over 50-percent of the trust assets managed by the local bank remain invested in Coca-Cola stock.

For decades Quincy's economy was supported by Coca-Cola dividends. The money kept people working when crops failed. It saved family homes when the national economy collapsed. In 1919 Coca-Cola's advertising said it was "the perfect answer." For many in Quincy that is what it became.

Chapter 12
Springfield, Missouri

A century of producing and selling Coca-Cola brought many changes to the bottling business as Coca-Cola grew to become the world's best known product. But what remained unchanged in Springfield, Missouri was the dedicated family making it happen.

The Rice family purchased the business in 1920 from the Electric Bottling Company which had started bottling sodas fifteen years earlier, with Coca-Cola as only a small portion of their business. They also produced a line of seven soft drinks called Farmer Beverages. The company was operating in the Producers Creamery & Produce building on west Phelps Street.

The family was living in Fulton, Kentucky where Edwin Rice, Sr. was a bank teller, when his brother Earl learned the Springfield business was for sale. All family members invested in the new bottling venture, unsure of what the next 100 years would hold. They moved to Springfield and the new corporation was formed by brothers Edwin, Earl and Richard along with their mother and

Edwin C. Rice, Sr.

Coca-Cola plant on Commercial Street

Coca-Cola plant on Clay Street

Tookie Heer

a fifth investor Dr. S. W. Paris who had been a druggist in Fulton.

For the first five years the Coca-Cola bottling continued at the previous owner's location, until the continued growth necessitated a move to a larger facility of west Commercial Street. Another move came nine years later to a new plant on north Clay Street which served the bottler well for the next forty-three years.

As the company grew the shareholders received as assets for their investment, individual territories within the franchise area. Dr. Paris became owner of the West Plains area, Earl and Edwin retained Springfield, Richard received Mountain Grove, and Edwin's sister Pearl received Bolivar. During that time Edwin's son Ed "Cookie" Rice Jr. and his wife Virginia became shareholders. "Cookie" was elected to the board in 1950 and became president in 1970. His oldest sister Tookie had married Ed Heer who joined the company and became secretary in 1950.

Throughout their 100 years Ozarks Bottling has always maintained their own bottling operation, and like other bottlers their production was reduced during WWII due to sugar rationing. However, a hospital to provide care for injured soldiers, O'Reilly General was built in Springfield, and Ozarks Bottling was allotted additional sugar to meet the new needs of the medical facility.

Called "The Hospital with a soul" it was built on the site of the Springfield Municipal Golf Course, which the city donated to the army. The hospital was built in four months at a cost of nearly two million dollars. During its five years of operation it served over 100,000 patients. In addition, an adjacent building called the "Castle" was purchased by the army from the Missouri Knights of Pythias. The Castle was converted into the enlisted men's club with a ballroom, bowling alley and gymnasium. Part of the basement became a medical care facility for war prisoners.

O'Reilly General Hospital

Ozarks Bottling began filling plastic bottles in 1973 in eight different sizes from 12oz to two liters. In 2019 the company added a new $18 million blow-molding bottle production line to triple production of the PET bottles. Bottled products also are sold to other Coca-Cola distributors who do not have the bottling capabilities. A new canning line is being developed at Ozark Bottling along with plans to bottle Dasani water.

After forty-three years Ozarks Coca-Cola/Dr. Pepper bottler needed more space, and a location was selected and building constructed in 1977 on North Packer Road. A large addition was constructed in 2019 with a 430,000 sq. ft. warehouse adjacent to the plant. A modern conveyor system

Coca-Cola plant on North Packer Road

connects the structures.

The company acquired the Coca-Cola business in Rolla, Missouri in 1979 and in 1987 the Dr. Pepper franchise was purchased from the Garland Reynolds family. Production of the beverage was moved to a new company plant on N. Packer road, and the former Dr. Pepper building was donated to Ozark Technical College in Springfield.

By 2014 Ozarks Coca-Cola was a top 10 bottler, and in 2015 and 2017 its franchise territory was expanded by acquisitions from the Coca-Cola Company. The new areas included Joplin and West Plains, Missouri as well as northwest Arkansas which includes the cities of Fayetteville and Bentonville. To serve the multi-state area the company has distribution centers in West Plains, Bolivar and Joplin and in Lowell, Arkansas.

Ozarks Bottling observed two important dates in Coca-Cola history in Springfield. The first in 2005 marked the 100th anniversary of Coke first being bottled there, and the second in 2020 paid tribute to the 100th year of the Rice family's ownership and local operation of the business. As part of the tribute Arkansas Governor Mike Parson and state representative Craig Fisher toured the plant with Cookie Rice

Edwin Rice, Jr. and his sister Tookie Heer with old delivery truck in 2005 as part of "Centennial Celebration," 100 years of Coca-Cola bottling in Springfield.

A company celebration in 2020, paying tribute to 100 years of Coca-Cola bottling by the Rice family in Springfield.

and viewed a recently installed new bottling line.

The company's history also is honored by a display of memorabilia in the lobby, and a larger display is being planned for the Springfield History Museum. Cookie's daughter and board chairperson Sally Hargis also planned a community open house celebration for the recent large plant addition.

With over 750 employees in four states Ozarks Coca-Cola/Dr. Pepper has been described as a "valuable asset to the region's manufacturing and distribution industry."

Hargis said her family's business is thankful for the community and proud to give back "through recycling programs and sustainability initiatives, and through work with local and national charities to have a positive impact on the community that shaped us as a company."

Chapter 13
Coca-Cola Christmas: Springfield, Tennessee

Christmas and Coca-Cola has become an annual tradition which creates special holiday memories, and at a former Coca-Cola plant in Springfield, Tennessee, Christmas memories are made even brighter.

Coca-Cola first called upon Santa Claus in 1910 hoping the popular Christmas figure would encourage customers to enjoy Coca-Cola during the holiday season. In 1931 advertising artist Haddon Sundbloom was hired by Coca-Cola to design a new Santa image, the first of many he ultimately would create. His Santa designs would appear on everything from Coca-Cola cans to decorations, cards, signs and even sweaters. The U.S. Postal Service selected four of the Coca-Cola Santas to appear on the holiday postage

Artist Haddon Sundbloom

First Santa for Coca-Cola, 1931

stamps in 2018.

Another Coca-Cola tradition was born in 1965 when Coca-Cola sponsored the first of what would become an annual favorite "A Charlie Brown Christmas" TV show.

A third holiday tradition was created in 1995 by a television advertisement which introduced the now familiar Coca-Cola Christmas trucks.

The decorated and brightly lit trucks now coming rolling in every holiday to communities throughout the United States, England, Australia and other countries.

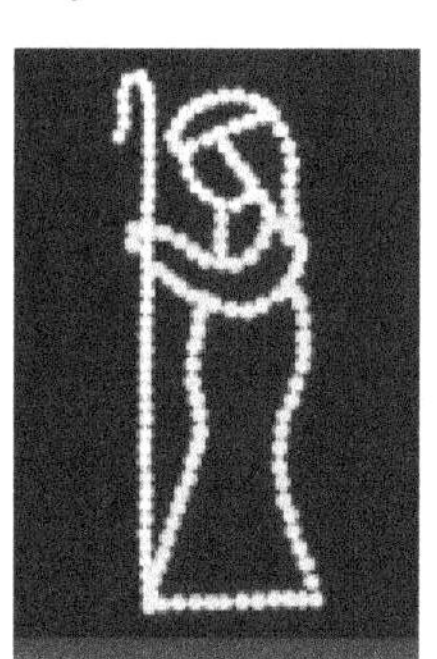

But in Springfield, Tennessee there are Christmas attractions unique to just that city and a former Coca-Cola bottling plant. It's called "Christmas Done Bright," a company which lights up the holidays by

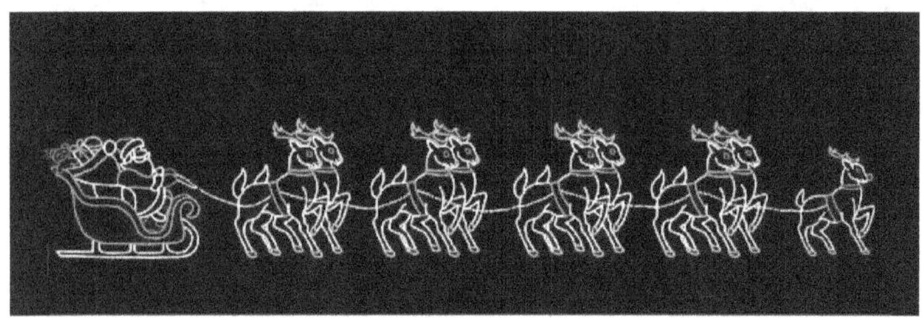

creating LED outdoor Christmas decorations. Founded in 1992 the family business is one of the first to manufacture affordable outdoor lighted decorations for both residential and commercial displays.

John and Linda Carley, their son Brad and daughter Melissa Davis started making the decorations in their home basement in Greenbrier about 15 miles southeast of Springfield. The business grew quickly and within eight years they had relocated to a 20,000 square foot former woolen mill building in Springfield. Nearby was the old Coca-Cola plant which had been unoccupied since Coca-Cola Bottling Consolidated had moved to a new location in 1998.

Again the owners of Christmas Done Bright realized they needed even more space, and in 2001 purchased the old plant which allowed them to expand their variety of outdoor decorations, lights and animated displays.

Coca-Cola had built the plant in 1940 and a few reminders of that previous use remained including an old large company safe which could not be opened because the combination was not known. The building's second floor had provided space for advertising, empty cases and the Coca-Cola syrup. No major renovations

Linda and John Carley

were required for the building's new use. The former bottling area became offices, and a separate room was used to display Coca-Cola memorabilia which had been donated or acquired.

During the 2019 holiday season the Christmas Done Bright building

Christmas Done Bright second location in Sevierville

appropriately was included on the annual Christmas tour of homes sponsored by the Robertson County Historical Society. The former plant became a popular stop on the tour with many visitors sharing personal memories from the Coca-Cola bottling days. The owners of Christmas Done Bright opened a second store in Sevierville, Tennessee.

The Coca-Cola Bottling Company was first licensed in Springfield in 1919, although there is some indication Coke may have been bottled there as early as 1908. By the mid 1920s records show the Coca-Cola Bottling Works had a new address on South Main Street, across from the L&N passenger depot.

Plans were made to construct a new facility in 1939 at an estimated cost of $70,000. The new plant, which later became the home for the Christmas lights business, was recognized with a three day open house event, September 12-14, 1940.

Chapter 14
Santa Fe: Peanuts In Your Coke

Peanuts in your Coke is a southern tradition which started in the early 20th century when cold bottled Coca-Cola and small bags of salted peanuts were starting to be sold at country stores and filling stations. Tearing off the corner of a small bag of peanuts created a funnel for pouring the contents into a bottle of Coke, and the sweet and salty taste quickly caught on.

However, for James A. Hart in Santa Fe, New Mexico salted peanuts also became an important ingredient in his first marketing efforts when he began bottling Coca-Cola in 1919. That simple idea grew to become a tradition for many years at Coca-Cola Bottling of Santa Fe.

James had first become interested in Coca-Cola as a business while working as an apprentice electrician in Albuquerque where he had been called to service the local Coca-Cola bottling plant. Later he moved to Santa Fe for a new opportunity and in December of 1919 used his first earnings to purchase the area's Coca-Cola franchise.

Brother Eugene joined James and together, with a foot-powered machine in James' garage they produced Coca-Cola and 14 other flavors of

James Hart's 1920 garage Coca-Cola plant

sodas. To introduce the new Coca-Cola James took one of the first cases to Kaunes Food Store and left it there on consignment saying he would return in a week to be paid for the bottles sold. When he returned the case was still full and was being used as a door stop.

That failed sales experience led to the "peanuts plan." James realized his new beverage needed to be sampled, and he also knew thirst was a good motivator. The two brothers bought a 50-pound bag of salted peanuts, and the youngsters packaged them into small single portion bags. For every bag of peanuts produced James and Eugene would make two bottles of Coca-Cola, with both peanuts and Coke then taken to be sold at high school football games. The peanut purchase would be followed by a Coca-Cola purchase by a now thirsty football fan.

The tasty combination of peanuts and Coke continued as a favorite Santa Fe tradition for decades. In the 1950s and 60s James' son Robert and his truck filled with bottles of cold Coca-Cola and bags of peanuts became a familiar and welcome addition to football games and other area events. His young daughter Kathy often accompanied Robert to help with the sales.

Looking back brought a reminder that

there was no truck to be used during those first years of bottling in 1919. Deliveries were made in an old wagon pulled by a faithful horse named "Ike." However, within two years the hard work started to bring returns and Ike was retired to be replaced by a model T Ford.

By 1923 the bottling company was serving a list of more than 50 customers, including the first one, Kaune's Grocery which through the years has remained one of the company's best customers.

The Coca-Cola bottling was moved from the original garage operation to a new store location in 1925. The new facility was constructed from rocks which helped reduce the concern of summer heat affecting the operation.

The third company relocation came in 1942 to a larger plant with offices and expanded warehouse space. During the following twenty years the facility was expanded three times.

World War II sugar rationing came after that move and the company discontinued

Horse and wagon delivery, 1919

Joe Black driving a model T Ford, 1925

Second Coca-Cola plant, 1925

Delivery trucks, 1937

Third Coca-Cola plant, 1939

bottling flavored drinks to concentrate only on Coca-Cola. "Sprite" was introduced in Santa Fe in 1961 and the diet drink "Tab" was added to the line in 1963.

With more products and ever-increasing demand, the need for additional space again became apparent. Construction for a new plant began in 1967 and by 1968 the company had completed the move to a new 27,000 square foot facility. That plant was expanded in 1980 with 10oz and 16oz bottles being filled there until 1992.

James' son Robert became manager of the new plant. Another son Albert and daughter Joann also assumed management positions. The family's Coca-Cola legacy has continued for more than a century, with six generations involved in both the business and the community's way of life in northern New Mexico.

The company's century mark anniversary was recorded in 2019 with a custom limited-edition Coca-Cola bottle. A display of old bottles, vending machines and other memorabilia can be viewed in the plant's lobby area at 660 W. San Mateo. You may be treated to a Coke, but you'll have to bring your own bag of peanuts.

James and Eugene Hart during the plant's 50th anniversary observance

Chapter 15
Coca-Cola Artist

Through the years Coca-Cola often is credited with creating a special memory. But for one person it also provided the inspiration for a rewarding and successful life.

Jim Harrison was only 14 years old when he first helped paint a Coca-Cola outdoor sign. He was a high school student in Denmark, South Carolina, when he took a summer job as an apprentice to an elderly sign painter, J.J. Cornforth, and they painted that first sign on the

Jim Harrison

side of a local hardware store. Soon the two were traveling the rural area painting the popular Coca-Cola murals on the sides of stores, barns and other structures. A lifelong admiration for the Coca-Cola logo evolved, and that trademark remained his favorite subject as Jim Harrison ultimately became recognized as one of America's foremost landscape artists.

His passion was to preserve the history of rural America, where he had been raised. Included in his paintings are country stores, railroad stations, schools, churches, farm buildings and even covered bridges.

A Coca-Cola mural painted on a country store in 1955 by Jim and Cornforth, was faded but still visible twenty years later, when Harrison featured the old store in one of his rural paintings.

He titled the painting "Disappearing America," and it was released as one of his first prints. The limited edition of 1500 copies became an immediate success and quickly sold out at $40.00 each.

It is believed to be the first Coca-Cola collector print to be put on the market, and has a current value of over $4,000.

He considered them subjects which needed to be captured on canvas.

He once said, "with my paintbrush I sometimes feel like I'm just one step in front of the wrecking ball."

Through the years Coca-Cola remained his inspiration, as he

Jim Harrison surrounded by his collection

also became an avid collector. Old signs, vending machines and other memorabilia were accumulated in his studio.

He entered into a licensee relationship with Coca-Cola in 1995, and Harrison created the artwork for the famous annual calendars, as well as other trademark products including trays, sun catchers, and canvas transfers.

In capturing those images of rural history, Harrison explained he wanted to communicate with the "common man of the street, the person who had little knowledge of art, but instead knew what he liked."

That connection was apparent in 2003 when a local businessman purchased from Harrison, a collection of 59 original Coca-Cola paintings, which at that time had an estimated value of over $1 million. In making the purchase, Donald Brandt explained he was not an art expert, simply a person who knew what he liked.

Brandt had been a fan of Harrison's work for years. He

The 2017 Coca-Cola Calendar is the last calendar personally prepared by Jim. The 11" x 13" wall calendar is a cherished collectible which features the artist's favorite subject, days gone by in rural America.

Donald Brandt with Jim Harrison

Donald Brandt with the Coca-Cola art collection

said, "I was raised in the country and many of the scenes Jim painted are familiar and bring back memories."

When Brandt learned the collection was available he considered it an opportunity to acquire a piece of area history, and also as an investment for his family. Brandt arranged for the collection to be stored in a vault at a local bank.

The Coca-Cola art collection represented about six years of Harrison's work. He said he had mixed emotions about parting with the paintings, but was consoled by the knowledge they would remain close to home.

The paintings had been in storage for a few years, and Harrison wanted to sell them as a collection, rather than individual paintings. It was reported as "the largest sale of Coca-Cola art in the history of Coca-Cola."

Jim Harrison died in June of 2016 at the age of 80. He was found dead of an apparent heart attack in his office. His work remains on display and available at the Jim Harrison Gallery, 4716 Carolina Highway in Denmark.

The gallery features Harrison prints, as well as bronzes, etchings, books and calendars. Open to the public Tuesday, Thursday and Friday; 10am to

5pm; Saturday 9am to 2pm; and other days by appointment. The gallery's phone number is 803-793-5796.

Jim Harrison Gallery

The gallery building is easily recognized by the large Coca-Cola mural painted on an outside wall.

Jim Harrison was an acclaimed artist receiving national and international awards for his work. In his home state he was honored in 2008 with the "Order of the Palmetto," which is South Carolina's highest civilian honor. The state transportation department has designated an intersection in Denmark as "Harrison Crossroads."

It's an ironic note to Harrison's life, that while in high school he had been recognized as the "class artist," but admitted he did not see a future career as an artist.

At the University of South Carolina he pursued a dual major in his two loves, art and physical education; and after graduation had a successful eleven year high school coaching career.

However, in the mid 1960's an art teacher encouraged him to pursue his desire and develop his art ability. He turned down a coaching position at Furman University, to return home to Denmark and the art career that followed.

Harrison's paintings today are proudly display in numerous personal and corporate collections including the Coca-Cola Company in Atlanta, The Maytag Corporation in Iowa, Philip Morris Corporation in New York, and the Augusta National Golf Club in Augusta, GA.

Chapter 16
Greenville, South Carolina

An old Coca-Cola plant, saved from demolition because of its unique architectural features, has become a valuable part of a multi-million dollar cultural center in Greenville, South Carolina. The Heritage Green Cultural Center is home to a collection of buildings which include the Greenville Hughes Public Library, The Upstate History Museum, and the Carolina Music Museum, which is located in the former Coca-Cola plant.

The 69-year-old Italiante style structure had been earmarked for demolition during early planning for the community's culture center. But the

Photo courtesy of Greenville County Library System

Photo courtesy of Greenville County Library System

unique style which included a tile roof, the original ornate brackets and down-spouts, and unusual outside light fixtures contributed to a decision to save and restore the building. However, additions to the building made after 1931 were removed.

Greenville historian Judith Bainbridge had emphasized the the importance of the building, telling the center planners "it represented part of Greenville's architectural heritage, providing a sense of the city's past".

The elaborate two-story brick building had been built during the Great Depression, a time when most commercial construction had come to a standstill. The building opened November 17, 1930 with a formal celebration, followed by a week-long open house and tours. It was an important event, creating hope for an improved economy in Greenville.

Coca-Cola was first bottled in Greenville by Charles Ellis in 1902, and he remained president of his bottling company until his death in 1918. His widow Stella then ran the business until 1947, becoming one of the first women to head a Coca-Cola company. The popularity of Coca-Cola increased rapidly during those years forcing the company to relocate five times as it grew to become one of the largest Coca-Cola plants in the south.

Greenville also was unique in Coca-Cola bottling history because at one time there were two Coca-Cola bottling plants in the community. The second smaller plant was constructed in 1931 at the rural Verner Springs location, where Ellis had purchased 60 acres of land in 1901.

The second plant also manufactured flavored soft drinks, including Verner Springs ginger ale. The Coca-Cola produced with the water from Verner Springs had a slightly different flavor, which some customers preferred.

The property, widely landscaped to include seven ponds with fish and wildlife became a favorite Greenville location for picnics, parties and community events.

Meanwhile, the convenient downtown location of the original plant made it popular for business and other social events. The Coca-Cola bottled downtown used water from Paris Mountain located about 8 miles north of Greenville where a reservoir provided the source of water for the city.

The Verner Springs plant was forced to close after World War II began, due to a shortage of both sugar and manpower. The site was given to the park district for use as a public park, but was abandoned in 1961 after the building burned down.

Charles Ellis's grandson, Waddy Anderson was the last Coca-Cola manager in Greenville. He retired in 1982 and Coca-Cola Consolidated of Charlotte bought the business. The Greenville operation was closed in 1998 when it was moved to Mauldin.

After a series of ownership changes, the old Coca-Cola building was restored to become home for the Carolina Music Museum in 2018. The museum is home to the

Hughes Main Library

Upcountry History Museum

world famous Clavier collection of over 40 English, European and American pianos and harpsichords dating from 1570 to 1845. Other culturally important instruments and musical performances also are part of the museum.

The new Hughes main library was constructed at the center at a cost of $17.8 million, made possible by a large donation from the Hughes brothers in honor of their parents. The new library opened in 2002 and is the hub for the entire Greenville library system. The former library building was renovated at a cost of $8 million to become a new children's museum.

Another new structure at the culture complex is the Upcountry History Museum which is a partnership with Furman University. The museum opened to the public in 2007 and has as its mission the promotion of history of the area's 15 counties.

A visit to the former Coca-Cola plant in Greenville also opens the door to an exciting world of history at the city's Heritage Green Cultural Center.

Chapter 17
Jellico, Tennessee

Childhood Coca-Cola memories may have served to motivate a businessman in Jellico, Tennessee to save his hometown Coca-Cola plant from demolition. Like many youngsters Johnny Baird watched through the large plant window as the Coca-Cola bottles were being filled. To add to the experience, often a bottling line worker would open a bottle of Coke to be enjoyed by the young fans outside, with the empties to be quickly returned.

The Coca-Cola building in Jellico remains as a survivor from the eight plant bottling empire created by pioneer Coca-Cola bottler Patrick Roddy, Sr. of Knoxville. Roddy and his initial business partner, William

Roddy-Goodman delivery truck

Goodman, a Knoxville candy maker, began bottling Coca-Cola in 1902. Their first plant in Knoxville was just the seventh franchise to be granted for Coca-Cola bottling.

The Roddy-Goodman Company established Coca-Cola plants in Middlesboro, Kentucky and Johnson City, Tennessee before building the Jellico plant in 1914.

The plant initially was a three story structure, but the third floor was destroyed by a fire in the 1950's. One of those watching the fire that night was a boy named Bill Branam whose view was from inside his father's car, while his father, the Jellico Fire Chief, battled the blaze.

Later, as a young man, Branam worked in the Coca-Cola plants in Jellico and Knoxville; and then for the Cavalier Company in Chattanooga which was a leading developer and manufacturer of Coca-Cola vending machines.

The first plant manager in Jellico was A. W. Griffin, who was with the Walla-Walla Chewing Gum Company in Knoxville, when hired by Roddy. Five years later Griffin also assumed the management position for Roddy's plant in Johnson City. He continued to live in Jellico but shuttled the 84 miles between the two plants, until moving to Johnson City in 1937.

Griffin's move opened the door for Mable Douglas to become manager in Jellico. Mable had started working at the plant in 1917 as bookkeeper, saying she would

Bill Branam

only stay a couple years. However, she remained for 52 years, serving as manager from 1937 until she retired in 1969. She had been manager when the plant burned, and saw the reconstruction to the current two-story structure. At that time truck loading bays were added to each side of the plant.

John Welch was plant manager from 1969 until retiring in 1973, when Jim Bollinger was reassigned from the Maryville plant to become Jellico's last manager. Bottling in Jellico was stopped in 1975 and plant was abandoned a year later. A distribution center in La Follette, about 15 miles away, then served the Jellico area. The La Follette facility was selected because it could accommodate the new larger trucks, which Jellico could not. Bollinger

remained manager and along with eight other employees, transferred to La Follette and were paid an allowance to cover travel expenses from their Jellico homes.

The old bottling equipment from the closed plant was cut up and sold as scrap. As many as one hundred old vending machines, signs, and other abandoned items were buried in a nearby strip pond, which had

Restoration work on the Jellico plant for future businesses.

been created by earlier coal mining.

The Jellico building remained empty for about five years before being purchased by Stirling Baird who operated a grocery store across the street and wanted to use the old building as a warehouse.

Stirling sold the decaying structure to his nephew Johnny Baird in 2009, and Johnny's childhood memories must have kicked in, as plans began to give the former Coca-Cola plant a new life. Restoring the building to its original unique appearance was the goal and Billy Douglas, who had a local home repair business, was selected for the task. Billy had worked in the plant in the 70s and eagerly accepted the restoration project.

Working with his son and another helper, it required nearly three years to achieve the goal and create a new home for Jellico businesses. Baird, a pharmacist, moved his drug store into one end of the building. The local Farm Bureau Insurance Company occupied the other end, and a physical therapy office moved into the center of the structure.

After the restoration, Billy Douglas continued to take care of the building doing maintenance projects, and painting the structure twice.

Another Jellico Coca-Cola memory can be seen at the public library, where an old bottling machine is featured in an area history display.

Chapter 18
Coca-Cola Art: Not Just A Sign

An old Coca-Cola mural became the inspiration for an amazing oil painting and for a future mural which reflect the lives and talents of two Minnesota painters. The original mural was painted on a country store in 1939 by Les Kouba a teenaged sign painter who found work and received

Les Kouba (top) painted the Coca-Cola logo so many times that he could sketch it backwards and up-side-down, which he demonstrated here on a table cloth.

what he remembered as his "basic training" while traveling from town to town painting Coca-Cola signs on buildings and trucks.

That first mural was painted on the side of Henry's Corner Store located northeast of Kouba's hometown of Hutchinson, Minnesota. The mural later became the subject for an oil painting called "The Country Store" which Kouba painted in 1991. Described as an auto-biographical painting it depicts three stages of the artist's life; as a youngster observing the mural being painted, as the young painter on his ladder creating the mural, and fifty years later sitting on the store's front porch enjoying his hobby of carving duck decoys.

Kouba described his painting as "a pleasant echo of America as it used to be in times more quiet and simple, the next best thing to living life again." Limited edition prints of the painting were created and made available.

Being raised in rural Minnesota Kouba had a natural love of the outdoors. That love and his talent lead to Les Kouba becoming internationally known as one of the world's foremost wildlife artists. He was recognized as the founder of the wildlife art revival in the 1970s.

Early in his Coca-Cola sign painting days Kouba also was instrumental in changing the appearance of the Coca-Cola logo. Frank Robinson, who was bookkeeper for Coca-Cola inventor John Pemberton, gave Coca-Cola its name in 1886, and created the original script logo for which Coca-Cola received a U.S. trademark in 1893.

Kouba's change to the logo happened almost by accident. He had been hired by a bottler in Tifton, Georgia in 1932 to paint a Coca-Cola sign in the local ballpark. Kouba thought the logo was too heavy looking and needed more slant to the letters along with some shading. The bottler agreed to the changes, and after the sign was completed he was so pleased that he notified Coca-Cola officials in Atlanta. Several Coca-Cola representatives with cameras visited the ballpark to view the sign and take photos. A few days later they returned with a release form for Kouba to sign, which gave Coca-Cola the use of the new logo design. Kouba received a sizeable fee for his work and later commented the experience had taught him to "never be afraid to try something new."

Kouba's talent and passion for something new contributed to his successful art career which included world wide recognition for his wildlife art, a prominent advertising art business, and for the creation of new art techniques.

Years later Kouba's Country Store painting was memorialized when a new mural was painted in his hometown by another Coca-Cola artist from Hutchinson who was a long time admirer of Kouba's work. David Wegscheid had first reproduced a Kouba picture when in his 9th grade oil painting class. Like Kouba, Wegscheid also painted Coca-Cola signs early in his career.

David opened a local

David Wegscheid with a print of Les Kouba's painting used to create his mural. Photo courtesy of Hutchinson Leader

Photos courtesy of Hutchinson Leader

sign shop in 1994 and although he had never met Kouba, the idea of honoring the fellow artist and hometown native had been on his mind for several years. He wanted to create on a prominent downtown site a full size mural replica of the famous "Country Store" painting.

Wegscheid shared his goal with Dave Kramer, owner of the downtown Ace Hardware store who gave his support to the proposal. Next local support helped fund the project and official approval was granted by the city council and the public arts commission.

The large 18ft x 14ft one-of-a-kind mural was unveiled on October

7, 2017, a date which observed the 100th anniversary of Kouba's birth. Viking Coca-Cola, the area bottler, helped fund the mural and sponsored the unveiling with free Coca-Cola and snacks.

Les Kouba is remembered for his wildlife art, for his paintings of hunting, and for capturing scenes of historic rural America. He accidentally also became interested in the number 13, and from that time forward 13 items would be found in most of his paintings. His stylized signature included 13 geese in flight. Kouba died on the 13th of September 1998.

An unplanned tribute to the artist took place just before the new mural was unveiled, when spectators observed a flock of 13 geese fly overhead. Wegscheid believed it was a sign of approval and thanks for what he had accomplished.

Kouba's hometown museum also pays tribute to the Coca-Cola painter who became an internationally acclaimed artist. The McLeod County Historical Museum's exhibit "Minnesota's Dean of Wildlife Art" proudly features the largest collection of Kouba's original artwork, limited edition prints, memorabilia and his art related inventions. It includes works from his high school days, as well as larger than life murals

from his early sign painting days; those days when he also added the Les Kouba touch to the classic Coca-Cola logo.

Kouba's famous upside down, backwards painting of the logo also is on display along with other Coca-Cola memorabilia at another Minnesota museum located about 35 miles away in Buffalo, Minnesota. The Veit Automotive Foundation is headed by Vaughn Veit who obtained the logo during a local college fund raising event. Kouba often participated in these type of events and would donate his Coca-Cola logo after creating it on a convenient table cover.

Veit's foundation maintains four museum display buildings with a primary theme of antique autos and related memorabilia. The foundation's "Long Barn" showroom is a 4,000 sq ft building which contains Coca-Cola advertisements and prints from Les Kouba.

Nearby is the "Round Barn" which was modeled after the popular old Round Barn on historic route 66. This building houses displays of

restored fuel pumps and Coca-Cola coolers. Included is a very rare
1947 American Vendor model 120.
Veit often discovered the Coca-Cola memorabilia while investigating
old filling station sites.

Veit also owns what is
believed to be the largest collection
of Coca-Cola trays featuring
actress and movie star Verna Clair.
Born Josephine Carroll French in
1914 in Senatobia, Mississippi,
she was only 6 years old when her family moved to Los Angeles where
she began modeling at the age of 16. Her first Coca-Cola tray image was
the "Running Girl" when she was 23 years old. She posed for additional
Coca-Cola trays for several more years and the museum's display features

Vaughn Veit holding Coca-Cola tray featuring actress Verna Clair

twelve of them, which are signed by Josephine.

Veit had met the actress during a visit to her ranch in California and during subsequent visits was able to obtain her signature on the trays which he had located during his museum searches for memorabilia. Josephine remained prominent in community affairs and died at the age of 98 in 2013 at a California retirement home.

The Veit Automotive Foundation display buildings, located at 8552 Baker Avenue NW in Buffalo, are open to visitors during the summer months.

Chapter 19
Lubbock, Texas

Lubbock Coca-Cola plant in 1938

A variety of Texas wines now are the beverage of choice at a former Coca-Cola plant in Lubbock's historic downtown depot entertainment district. The last bottle of Coca-Cola left that Texas plant in 1963.

The unique structure was built in 1938 in an attractive Streamline Moderne architectural style which features huge curved and glass block windows. After Coca-Cola moved to a new facility on the city's east side, the old plant building was leased to several different businesses until 2007 when it caught the attention of internationally known wine maker Kim McPherson.

Kim McPherson making wine

A former wine-maker at Caprock Winery south of Lubbock, McPherson had over 16 years experience and was seeking a new challenge. Caprock had grown and he was looking for a smaller facility in downtown Lubbock where he could produce about 8,000 cases of wine.

McPherson credits his father with providing his inspiration to produce wines. Clint "Doc" McPherson, a chemistry professor at Texas Tech, had founded the Llano Estacado winery also located near Lubbock, which had become known as the largest, best selling premium winery in Texas. Both he and his father have been inducted into the Texas Food and Wine

The winery under construction

The winery tasting room

Hall of Fame. Kim's wines have won over 400 medals in state, national and international competitions. The McPherson family has been part of Texas grape growing and wine making for over 40 years.

Kim said the new winery provided an opportunity to do what he always wanted, to produce several types of Texas wines. "This is where the best grapes are grown" he said, "it is our mission to grow and make wines with a real sense of place, the Texas high plains."

When the former Coca-Cola plant became available, McPherson seized the opportunity because of the building's historic location and the quality of the Lubbock water supply. He said it was the best decision he could have made and spent the next year with his staff and contractors creating a full-scale winery on the half-block downtown site. The winery opened in the fall of 2008, featuring a tasting room, an events center, an outdoor patio and a fountain utilizing Coke bottles and other artifacts. Kim McPherson continues to play an innovative role in the development of the Texas wine industry.

Coca-Cola apparently was first bottled in Lubbock in 1905 according to sparse records in the Coca-Cola archives. No local information about the early bottling could be located except for a 1920 advertisement in the Lubbock Avalanche newspaper which promoted daily soda production at the Lubbock Creamery. The notice listed the availability of at least a dozen drinks including Coca-Cola, Delaware Punch and Green River.

However, five years after that first advertisement was published, the Coca-Cola area franchise was officially awarded to the Coca-Cola Bottling Company of Lubbock which marked the beginning of the bottling business for generations of another Coca-Cola family.

It all started when John McNamara was selling Coca-Cola in the 1920s at his soda fountain in Austin, and his wife enjoyed the drink and encouraged John to become more involved with the beverage. What

*Photographs courtesy of Special Collections Library,
Texas Tech University*

followed next was a meeting in Atlanta where John learned that Coca-Cola franchises for Lubbock and Plainview were the only two remaining available in Texas. He made an offer for both franchises which was accepted a few days later and John opened the plants in both cities. His sons, Carl and Pat McNamara who were living in Dallas, were put in charge of the new bottling business.

Coca-Cola bottling in Lubbock got started in an old building formerly called the "Oprey House" which also was owned by John McNamara. The building had been built at Texas and 14th street in 1905 for community events and entertainment. A newspaper advertisement in 1927 stated Coca-Cola for sale at area grocers for $1.00 per case plus 75-cents deposit for the bottles. By 1928 more space was needed for Coca-Cola bottling and John had the old "Oprey House" structure replaced with a new two-story brick building.

Forrest L. Lindsey was plant manager in Lubbock in 1937 when plans were announced for another new plant, this one to be constructed in the 1600 block of Texas Avenue. The two-story 50 by 125 foot structure would accommodate offices and production with adjacent space for future expansion. Seventy years later that same building became the home for McPherson Cellars.

Growth continued for Lubbock Coca-Cola, and in 1941 the manager boasted the business had twenty-seven employees and fifteen trucks serving a nine-county area.

However a year later, like all other Coca-Cola plants, production was drastically reduced when WWII sugar rationing went into affect. Lindsey said bottling was reduced by almost half the usual amount, and he added that four or five of his employees were joining the army. Among them was John McNamara's son Carl J. who had been with the Lubbock operation since it started.

The business felt the war effort in other ways as well. A shortage of bottles caused the company to place advertising to encourage customers to return their empties. The plant's delivery trucks often were followed by cars carrying local shoppers who wanted to be first to purchase at the grocery stores where Coca-Cola allotments had been reduced. Lubbock's Coca-Cola delivery men also responded to a nation wide request from the war department to collect donations of musical instruments which were shipped to servicemen overseas.

After the war the company built a much

needed truck and storage facility at a different location. It also marked the installation of the first Coca-Cola vending machine which would make change during the purchase.

Once again Lubbock's Coca-Cola bottling needed more space, and in 1963 a 60,000 sq ft plant was built on the east side of town. The facility had 135 employees and the latest bottling equipment, including a new bottle washer which manager Lindsey boasted was the largest in Texas. Pat McNamara Jr. had joined the company in 1959 and was serving as sales manager when the new plant was opened with a day long community celebration on April 23rd.

Pat became president in 1972 and company growth followed with Coca-Cola franchises being acquired in Monahans, Texas and in New Mexico at Rosewell, Clovis, Alamagordo, Hobbs and Carlsbad. Pat also was elected president of the 500 member Texas Soft Drink Association.

Lubbock Coca-Cola plant in 1963. Photograph courtesy of the City of Lubbock

The new Coca-Cola plant survived one of the worst tornados in Texas history in May of 1970, and also experienced a freak act of nature remembered by area historians. Over $200 million in damage was done in the central business district, with over 500 people injured and another 26 killed. Also a reminder of that storm's power was its passing over the Coca-Cola plant where cases of full bottles were waiting to be shipped. The tornado's low pressure sucked the soda out of the bottles, while leaving the empties with caps still on top.

Pat's son, Patrick McNamara III became a manager in Lubbock in 1982, and a year later took charge of the company's plant in Clovis. Four years later the entire McNamara Coca-Cola operation was sold to Ed Hoffman of Coca-Cola Southwest. Hoffman's company had been acquiring plants throughout Texas and became the 5th largest bottler in the nation. But just two years later Coca-Cola bought all of the Hoffman plants and territory for $1.1 billion.

Two decades later Pat McNamara III visited his former Lubbock Coca-Cola plant, which had become the McPherson winery. He reminisced with Kim McPherson about watching the Cokes being bottled. Pat had become a senior vice-president at Southern Glazer's Wine and Spirits in Dallas, the nation's largest distributor of wine and spirits. Ironically one of the products sold by Southern Glazer's is the wine made at McPherson Winery.

Chapter 20
Statesville, North Carolina

A restored Coca-Cola mural created a special memory for a North Carolina town and for the young painter who brought the sign back to life.

Murals were prominent on many downtown buildings in Statesville, North Carolina in the early to mid 1900's. But by 2018 only one was still slightly visible. That old Coca-Cola mural is located on the side of a large building occupied by Roots Outdoor at 201 W. Broad Street. The building's owner, Brett Powers, along with the Downtown Statesville Development Corporation, convinced both city officials and bottling giant Coca-Cola Consolidated to restore the badly faded sign.

The request was not unusual to the Charlotte bottler, as they had been dedicated to bringing "ghost signs" back to life for the past few years. Coca-Cola Bottling Company Consolidated is the largest independent Coca-Cola bottler in the United States.

However, the Statesville project not only brought back memories for many residents, it also brought back special family memories for the young artist who

Amber Thompson and Andy Thompson in Concord

Amber Thompson and Andy Thompson in Cherryville

was selected to do the work.

Amber Thompson's first Coca-Cola sign experience came after graduating from college in 2016, when she had the opportunity to work with her grandfather Andy Thompson. Andy had become a Coca-Cola legend while painting signs for nearly sixty years for Coca-Cola Consolidated.

Amber credits her grandfather for teaching her "the ropes of sign painting". She remembers those intern days when the two of them painted murals in Concord and Cherryville before Andy died in 2017. She described the Statesville mural restoration as a special "labor of love," an opportunity to carry on her grandfather's legacy.

Amber previously had done other projects for Consolidated, including a corporate lobby mural and a large conference table. She said she is looking forward to other projects, including a Coca-Cola mural in Charlotte where she would give new life to an old sign originally created by her grandfather.

The Statesville restoration had special meaning for the downtown development organization as well. Association Executive Director Marin Tomlin said the mural "brings back to life" a part of the city's history and creates community pride. The mural was officially dedicated April 13, 2019 with a large gathering of local officials and representatives of Coca-Cola Consolidated to witness the ribbon cutting.

Amber Thompson restoring the Statesville, North Carolina mural.

Coca-Cola was first available in Statesville in 1896 as a fountain drink at Hall's Drug Store. The first bottled Coca-Cola became available in 1902 after J. Luther Snyder opened one of the state's first bottling plants about 42 miles away in Charlotte. For the next seven years Snyder would travel to Statesville to take

Amber Thompson painting a corporate lobby mural.

Photos courtesy of Statesville Historical Collection

orders for Coca-Cola, which he filled at his Charlotte plant.

Two other North Carolina plants, Greensboro and Hamlet, also began operation in 1902, and those three plants formed the nucleus for today's Coca-Cola Bottling Company Consolidated of Charlotte.

Snyder opened the Statesville plant in 1909, and sent his cousin F. H. Snyder from Salisburg to become the manager. However, the cousin left about a year later, and in 1913 Snyder sold the business to Z. E. Murphy of Rocky Mount and S. C. Gates of Greenville.

The Johnson Coca-Cola legacy in Statesville, which lasted for more than six decades, began in 1916 when Frank L. Johnson moved from West Virginia to purchase the plant. He lead the operation during a period of rapid growth which twice included construction of new plants along with nu-

merous bottling inno-
vations. He also consid-
ered the addition of ice
cream manufacturing
for his business.

Within four years
Johnson announced
plans for a new two
story Coca-Cola plant,
which would be a brick
structure with a glass
front viewing win-
dow and new bottling

The Coca-Cola building with community hall on the 2nd floor.
Photo courtesy of Statesville Historical Collection

equipment. The business remained at that Court Street location for over a
dozen years.

However, growth again necessitated the need for more space, and in
1932 an even larger facility was opened which included a spacious second
floor community hall. The hall included a stage with curtains and a large
area for seating and other activities. For more than 25 years the hall served
as Statesville's community center, hosting business and civic events, as
well as social gatherings. The local scout troops met there, and there were
weddings, Christmas dinners and other special event observances.

Frank Johnson remained manager until his death in 1941. His son
James V. Johnson succeeded him in 1950, and ultimately became President
and CEO of Coca-Cola Bottling Company Consolidated.

The last Coca-Cola plant in Statesville was built in 1954. Located on
Taylorville Road, it was reported the plant "rivaled any bottling firm in
the state from the standpoint of equipment and service."

The old building which included the popular Coca-Cola hall was
closed, and ultimately it was converted into several business offices.

Bottling was continued for about twelve years at the new Taylorville
plant. However, in 1965 the facility was converted to serve for a brief
period as a distribution center for Coca-Cola Consolidated. In 2019 the

building was occupied by an industrial supply company.

The history of Statesville Coca-Cola is just a small part of Statesville history and photos which can be enjoyed at the "Statesville Historical Collection." The unique community museum is dedicated to promoting the understanding and preservation of area history.

Located at 212 S. Center Street, there is no admission fee and it is open Monday through Friday, Noon until 4 pm. Other times by appointment.

Managed by Steve Hill, a knowledgeable area historian, the museum is a "must stop" for visitors and history enthusiasts.

Chapter 21
Jefferson City, Missouri

A Missouri family has been in the beverage business in the state's capital city for over 130 years, and more than a century of that time has been focused on bottling and selling Coca-Cola.

It started in 1892 when Jacob Moerschel, a German immigrant bought the C & L Wagner Brewery in Jefferson City. The name was changed to Capitol Brewery, and his two sons Jacob W. and Ernst joined the business and ultimately became responsible for its operation.

The company became one of Missouri's earliest Coca-Cola bottlers in 1905. The first was started in St. Louis in 1902. The Jefferson City plant also bottled other flavored sodas including root beer, Squirt and Mellow Yellow.

The combined beer and soda business was doing well until 1920 when the federal Volstead act brought beer brewing to a halt. To help the company survive they started delivering ice and coal, providing cold storage facilities and expanded the soft drink business. Seeing the rapid growth of Coca-Cola the Moer-

schels acquired the area bottling franchise in 1922 which provided a central Missouri distribution area of fourteen counties.

When prohibition was repealed in 1933 brewing resumed for Capitol Brewery until 1947 when it shut down again, but this time permanently due to increasing competition in the beer industry in Missouri. The Moerschels constructed a new plant in 1941 to be used only for bottling Coca-Cola after there was concern that yeast from the brewing process might affect the Coca-Cola products.

The building was constructed of thick concrete walls allowing it to later be designated as a federal fallout shelter. During the "cold war" the shelters were established to provide protection from radioactive fallout in the event of a nuclear explosion.

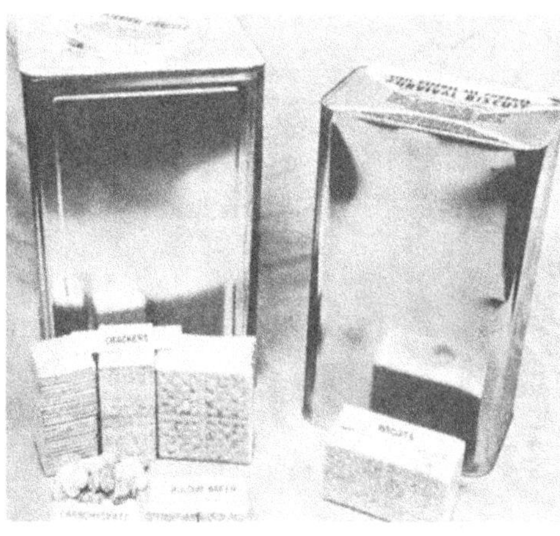

The Coca-Cola Bottling building received the Federal Fallout Shelter designation and stocked survival foods in it's basement during the 1960s.

The community fallout shelter program began in 1961 and buildings of solid construction like the Coca-Cola plant became shelter sites. They were marked with a standard yellow and black sign which remains today near the entrance. The plant's basement became the shelter area and was stocked with canned water, basic food needs and other supplies. Federal funding for the shelter program continued for about a decade.

The company changed its name to Jefferson City Coca-Cola Bottling in 1944, and bottling continued at the new plant until 2001. However that landmark structure continues as the company headquarters for sales and distribution for the entire franchise territory. The art-deco design building was designated a historic Landmark by the city in 2008. During the initial construction of the building a 485-feet deep well was drilled through bedrock to provide pure water for the bottling process. The well remains as the only water supply for the building. An engraved corner stone above the front entrance bears an inscription in memory and honor of Jacob W. Moerschel and Ernst C. Moerschel.

Ernst's daughter Rose Mary and her husband Carl F. Vogel became the 3rd generation to run the company. The family tradition continued with the fourth generation when their four children became involved. Carl M. Vogel served on the board and became President in 1983.

Carl also served in the Missouri General Assembly from 1991 to 2010, first as a member of the house for twelve years and then in the senate for eight years. His sister Emily Talken also was an active public servant being involved in several community organizations, as well as the area historical society and as president of the school board.

A highly visible example of the company's community support is a large changeable message sign which was constructed on the plant's roof in 1960. It was first a steel "ballpark like" structure where messages were changed manually, and then later up-dated to an electric board where advertising is easily provided for area activities. The popular sign is viewed from the U.S. highway 50 expressway and has been described as a "community symbol."

Upon the death of Carl Vogel his son Jacob became President in 2016 and represents the fifth family generation to head the business. Jacob foresees continued growth and community service for Jefferson City Coca-Cola and has plans for a Coca-Cola museum and store.

Chapter 22
The Last Bottle

The last returnable 6.5oz bottle of Coca-Cola was filled in October 2012 at a family owned Coca-Cola plant in Winona, Minnesota. What happened to that historic bottle?

It was sold at auction and successfully purchased that final day of bottling by Michael Faber of St. Cloud, Minnesota, who is President of Viking Coca-Cola Company. All of the 5,879 bottles filled that day included a commemorative neck wrap. Faber paid $2000 for his last bottle, while the remaining bottles were priced at $20 each, with the proceeds designated to support a Winona public trail project.

The last bottle was stored in a secure location, and eights years later Michael said he had been offered much more than the original price for his unique piece of Coca-Cola history. However, it was not for sale as he explained his reason for purchasing the bottle was to create a family Coca-Cola heirloom. Unlike many family bottlers who often accumulate decades of Coca-Cola memorabilia, the Fabers had just purchased Viking Coca-Cola in 1994.

Viking Coca-Cola also represents another one of the Coca-Cola success stories. Michael's father, Joe Faber had been a farmer when he started driving a Coca-Cola truck in 1962. He progressed to sales manager, and ultimately in 1966 he was selected as general manager. A small ownership position accompanied that new management position. During the following years Joe Faber was able to acquire financial support which made it possible to purchase the entire operation when it became available in 1994.

Michael remembered his father as always being optimistic, and that he continued to fight his own courageous battle with cancer during his years of managing and buying the company. Joe Faber lost that battle just a year after the purchase had been completed.

Viking Coca-Cola Bottling was formed by Howard Hamilton in 1952 in Brainerd, but the headquarters were relocated to St. Cloud when that plant was purchased in 1962. The business continued to expand and by 2020 had facilities in thirteen Minnesota and northwest Wisconsin cities.

Michael's two-hundred mile trip to the last bottling event came after he received a personal telephone invitation from Winona Coca-Cola President and General Manager LeRoy Telstad. Other area bottlers also had been invited and were joined by Coca-Cola officials, bottle and memorabilia collectors, and interested Coca-Cola fans from several states.

One of those guests to address the gathering was Randy Mayo, a Biedenharn descendent, who recalled that Coca-Cola was first bottled

Left to Right: Winona Coca-Cola Bottling Company officers LeRoy Telstad and Clinton A. Kuhlman; Phil Mooney Coca-Cola Chief Archivist presenting certificate in recognition of the last bottle run.

LeRoy Telstad holds the last bottle

by Joe Biedenharn on the southern banks of the Mississippi River in Vicksburg in 1894. Then 118 years later the last returnable bottle was filled on the river's northern bank in Winona. Coca-Cola Chief Archivist Phil Mooney also spoke at the event where he reviewed the history of the iconic Coca-Cola bottle.

The returnable Coca-Cola bottle was last produced in 1990, and to accomplish the final bottling run, as he had done before, LeRoy Telstad had to locate sources for the small bottles. That last bottle purchased by Michael Faber had been first filled in 1948 by a Coca-Cola plant in Minneapolis.

Thru the years of locating bottles, LeRoy also built a collection of bottles which represented 1,090 of the total 1240 locations where Coca-Cola had been bottled.

His bottle collection included 250 examples of those called the "Christmas bottle," which are dated 1916 and 1923 the years

when the now famous bottle design was first patented and then re-registered. It is believed 1916 marked the first time a U.S. patent was issued for a "consumer package."

In addition to the bottle collection an informal memorabilia museum is located in the plant's upper level storage area. It contains dozens of old vending machines, advertising and promotional material and old signs with some of them new and in original cartons. LeRoy will provide visitors a personal tour of the collection when he is available.

By 2020 a few dozen of the special bottles from the final run remained available, still at a cost of $20 each. The sale of the bottles had raised over $85,000 for the maintenance of the five-mile public trail along an oxbow of the Mississippi river.

Coca-Cola was first bottled in Winona in 1905 by the Winona Bottling Company which had been established earlier in 1870 by David Fakler who was succeeded in the business by his son William Fakler. When William died in 1904 George Hassinger became manager and also acquired half ownership from Fakler's widow.

The plant was producing Coca-Cola in 1906 when the Winona newspaper reported the drink was "becoming a local Favorite". Winona Bottling also was producing California Cider and another beverage not classified as a soft drink, called "Bromo Celery Tonic".

Two years later Winona Bottling was able to purchase and move into a two-story brick building previously owned by a printing company. The structure was remodeled to provide areas for both soda and beer bottling. In addition to Coca-Cola and flavored sodas, there was bottling of ginger ale and Erlanger beer. Serving a 30 mile radius of Winona with motor trucks, the company had become the largest bottler east of the twin cities.

Continued growth required another move in 1920 when the company secured a five-year lease on a building formerly used as a bottling plant by Park Brewing Company, which was forced to close because of prohibition.

Things changed for Coca-Cola in 1923 when the Conedale Spring Water bottling company was formed and purchased Winona Bottling.

Conedale co-owner Frank Landon said his company would only bottle soft drinks which used the spring water, and he would dispose of all Winona products including Coca-Cola. Landon owned the Conedale Farm which would provide the spring water.

For several years Coca-Cola was distributed in Winona by the Coca-Cola Bottling Company of Minneapolis. Owner Thomas J. Moore had obtained a "master franchise" for the entire state of Minnesota and eastern North Dakota. Meanwhile the ambitious plans of Conedale were failing and they were forced to merge with Wonderlick Brothers Bottling, which had succeeded in purchasing a full Coca-Cola franchise for $10,000 from Thomas Moore.

The beginning of more than eight decades of Coca-Cola bottling by the Kuhlman family began in 1933 when Clint A. Kuhlman purchased Wonderlick Bottling, changed the name to Coca-Cola Bottling Company of

Winona and constructed what became the plant's current home.

The business remained in the Kuhlman family and in 2020 the great granddaughter of Clint A., Cindy Telstad was Vice President, her husband LeRoy was President and her sister Kathi Fischer also served as a company officer.

Winona Coca-Cola faced many challenges during those more than 80 years as a family business, and like other businesses during WWII dealt with shortages of sugar and other products including items made of steel.

LeRoy Telstad recalled the difficulty his company had in obtaining bottle caps. Like some other bottlers, Winona Coca-Cola would be forced to collect used caps, which would be returned to the manufacturer to be recondition for use again on Coca-Cola bottles. The reconditioned caps

An early Coca-Cola delivery truck

were unique as they were painted gray. The reason for the single drab color was that red and yellow paint was difficult to obtain.

The actual Coca-Cola bottles also were affected by war shortages. The original bottles always had a green tint which was created by minerals in the sand which was used to make the glass. Bottle manufacturers who did not use sand with the mineral content had been adding copper to achieve the desired color. However, copper also was scarce and some bottles manufactured during the war were of clear white glass.

Chapter 23
Cuero, Texas

Will a former Coca-Cola bottling plant in Cuero, Texas become the home for a new Coca-Cola museum? A local historian and collector thought it should and in 2020 was working to make it happen.

William Adickes of Cuero had a special connection to the old building because it was built by his father in 1931. He also fondly remembered when he was six years old pressing his nose against the plant's large glass window to watch as the moving line of bottles were washed and filled with Coca-Cola. The bottling stopped when the business was sold to a larger bottler in San Antonio in 1985. The building remained vacant for several years and was starting to become a downtown eyesore until Adickes was instrumental in convincing the city council to buy the building in 2012. A 1960 addition to

the building was torn down after the purchase, and city manager Raymie Zella estimated a cost of about $1 million to renovate the remaining original structure.

Adickes then began to promote plans for the renovation to include the Coca-Cola museum in the front portion of the building which would display memorabilia he had acquired, along with other items donated by family members of the original bottler, former employees and others who learned about the museum plans. Unique among those items are three six-foot high Coca-Cola murals, still mounted on sheet rock which had been salvaged from the walls of the Coca-Cola plant in Victoria. The plant was a "sister plant" to Cuero, which also was closed and sold in 1985. The murals had been painted by Anthony Miculka, an artist from Cuero.

Adickes also remembered a 7-foot high neon bordered sign which had hung in front of the plant, but had disappeared several years after the closing. He hoped to locate the original sign or have one recreated from a drawing he had acquired. The large original sign post remained in front of the building, but no longer met city code requirements and had to be grandfathered in to be saved from removal.

Coca-Cola sign painter

A suggested use for the rear portion of the building was to establish a small fire equipment museum. Adickes said it would be a large enough area to display three old city fire trucks which were being restored. Also available were old fire department memorabilia including a three story high wooden ladder originally purchased to provide upper floor access to the court house.

Preserving area history is important to William Adickes as he served several years as board chairman of the Cuero Heritage Museum. During that time he was instrumental in the creation of a large permanent Coca-Cola exhibit which utilized many items from his personal collection. The Heritage Museum is located in the Federal Building which was built in 1915 and served for years as the Cuero post office.

The exhibit contains antique vending machines, signs, bottles and other memorabilia including one rare item from the 1940s which may be the only one known still to exist. Although not recognized as an official Coca-Cola product, it does display a Coca-Cola promotional tag, and it probably was used in restaurants where Coca-Cola was sold. Called the "Toas-Tite" electric sandwich maker, it was built and sold for about 20 years by the Bar-B-Buns Company of Cincinnati. The purpose of the kitchen-type appliance was to create indoors the type of popular sandwich which was being made over campfires with a hand held device. It's believed the electric units may have been used as a restaurant sales promotion by Coca-Cola.

The permanent museum display was created to honor Cuero Coca-Cola bottling

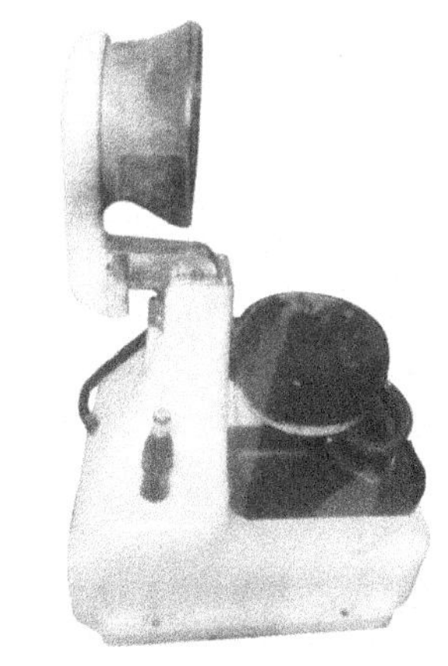

The Heritage Museum Coca-Cola exhibit includes this rare "Toas-Tite" electric sandwich maker.

which expanded to become a major economic contributor to the area.

There is additional Coca-Cola memorabilia located nearby in another Cuero city museum. Housed in an old pharmacy building constructed in 1889, is the Pharmacy and Medical Museum of Texas, and like most old time pharmacies it included a soda fountain. The museum has on display part of that soda fountain as well as an original Coca-Cola syrup dispenser. The ornate porcelain urn was made in 1896 for the Coca-Cola Company, and the urns supposedly were "loaned" to soda fountains which purchased at least 35 gallons of syrup the previous year. It's doubtful if many were ever returned to Coca-Cola, and now they remain a valued collector's item.

Original Coca-Cola syrup dispenser

Records indicate Coca-Cola was first bottled in Cuero in 1910, but the fascinating history of Coca-Cola in that city is the story of three generations of the Summers family, beginning in 1926.

E. T. Summers Sr. was born in 1894 in Slidell, Louisiana and first became involved with Coca-Cola in 1916 as a sales and delivery person for Louisiana Coca-Cola in New Orleans. Ten years later he became aware of the availability of three Tex-

E. T. Summers Sr. & Jr. with a delivery truck at Cuero plant

as plants; Cuero, Brownsville and Austin. His choice was Cuero because, he observed there were a lot of cotton pickers in the region and they drank a lot of Coca-Cola.

His son, E.T. Summers Jr. had his first Coca-Cola plant job at the age of 11 years where he washed bottles and helped on deliveries. He later took time off to graduate from the University of Texas and serve for three years during WWII in London and France. His brothers, Paul and Buddy also were involved in the business as they were responsible for the company's distribution facilities in Victoria and Port LaVaca.

Cuero Coca-Cola was involved in numerous community projects, but the most prominent was their support for the city's major annual event known as the "Turkey Trot." The festival started in 1912 as a way to promote south Texas turkey growers. The bottler always sponsored a float in the parade, but gained unexpected attention when a plant employee became a local celebrity. Production manager Roy Binz enjoyed entertaining as a clown and had become popular performing for children's shows and other events. Known as "Coco the Clown" he became a featured participant in the annual parade. His clown costume is

CoCo the Clown in Cuero Fire Department's Antique Fire Truck.

proudly included in the museum's Coca-Cola exhibit.

Like his father the third Summers family generation, E. T. "Toby" Summers started working in the plant as a youngster, with one of his first jobs the painting of wooden cases which held the bottles. Also like his father, Toby later graduated from the University of Texas with both a business and a law degree. He returned to Cuero and remained with Coca-Cola even after the plant was closed and territory sold to San Antonio Coca-Cola bottling.

San Antonio was one of several Texas plants owned by the Biedenharn family, and just a year later those plants were all sold to Ed Hoffman of Coca-Cola Southwest. The new company had been acquiring plants to become the nation's 5th largest bottler. Ownership change came one more time in 1988 when the Hoffman family sold all the Southwest operation to Coca-Cola for $1.1 billion.

Meanwhile Toby Summers had advanced to a management position by 1973, and under his leadership a new Coca-Cola venture was begun in Cuero. The popularity of Coca-Cola in cans was growing in the '70s and bottlers were joining together to build cooperative canning plants.

Toby Summers faced that challenge as well and in 1981 obtained support from two other Texas Coca-Cola bottlers to create the Crossroads Canning Company in Cuero. A 60,000 sq-ft plant was built and equipped to provide Coca-Cola in cans to several Texas plants owned by the canning company's partners.

Cuero Coca-Cola's partnership in Crossroads was included in the 1985 sales to San Antonio, and in the subsequent sales to Coca-Cola Southwest and Coca-Cola corporate. Throughout the rapidly changing ownerships of Crossroads canning, Toby Summers remained in management and another project was undertaken as the plant began the production of the actual syrup used in making Coca-Cola. Crossroads received syrup concentrate from Coca-Cola corporation to produce the finished product which was shipped to other bottling plants.

A third and final product to be produced at Crossroads required the plant be doubled in size in 1990. Toby had obtained a five-year contract for the bottling of a new and rapidly growing product line called "Clearly Canadian." The flavored water drink was made with water shipped to Cuero by rail from Canada.

Coca-Cola closed the Crossroads canning company in 1995. Toby Summers retired from Coca-Cola in 1999. His brother John, who also had remained in San Antonio, left six months later but continued the family name in Coca-Cola bottling as he joined the Nashville facility owned by Coca-Cola Consolidated. Then in 2003 he joined Meridian Coca-Cola to manage plants in Meridian, Mississippi and Union City, Tennessee.

The former canning plant in Cuero later was used as a furniture warehouse. Then the large building remained empty for years awaiting a new tenant and use. But it remains a reminder of how a small Texas city played a big role in Coca-Cola history.

Chapter 24
Save Our Signs
Parksley, Virginia

The quest to preserve and restore old Coca-Cola outdoor murals continues, as often those colorful works of sign art have become a valuable part of a community's history with special memories to be saved.

When a Virginia businessman bought an old grocery building in downtown Parksley in 2017, he quickly realized a faded Coca-Cola mural on an outside wall had to be saved. Tim Valentine, manager of the Club Car Cafe, purchased the nearby building as an investment and for possible future personal use. Valentine had lived in Parksley for over forty years and always admired the building.

Town residents had talked for years about the classic sign and the need to restore the fading image. However the required sign project had not been supported by the building's previous owner.

Tim knew the restoration had to be done soon, or the sign would

deteriorate to the point where it could not be saved. He first sought help from the Coca-Cola distributor for the area, Coca-Cola Consolidated of Charlotte. The bottler had become known for its "ghost sign" project, which was restoring dozens of area Coca-Cola murals. However, Tim learned there was a long list of signs waiting for the company painters, and it could be years before the Parksley mural would be considered.

He decided to take things into his own hands and hired two willing friends, David Parks and Billy Crockett, who assured him they would get the job done. The two men worked for several days in warm June weather and used a donated portable lift to reach the upper portions of the sign. When completed the 25-by-15 foot mural covered almost all of the side of the two story brick building.

The building first served the community for years as the Parksley Grocery Company. In the 1940's it became a five-and-dime store. A glass brick facade was added in 1950 when remodeling was being done by the Hopkins family who owned the building at that time.

For the next fifty years a state owned ABC liquor store was located there, with a tax service firm to become the next tenant. Finally in 2020 Valentine leased the lower level to a specialty food market and was considering options for use of the upper level.

But whatever those plans bring, the brightly restored Coca-Cola mural will be there to help create new memories for residents and visitors to Parksley, thanks to the quick action and determination of a new building owner.

SOS - Batesville, Virginia

The restoration of a century old Coca-Cola mural was a "dream come true" for residents of an Arkansas community and a rare educational opportunity for art students at the local liberal arts college.

For years the citizens in Batesville had been commenting on the poor and deteriorating condition of the large Sprite Boy sign. In addition a local planning survey revealed historic murals were considered an important asset of the community. Meanwhile the art students at Lyon College had created new murals at the park and for the sheriff's department, and this attracted the attention of Kyle Christopher, Tourism Director for the chamber of commerce. He and college art professor Dustyn Bork met and agreed on a plan for the mural's restoration. Christopher then began the task of organizing community support.

Coca-Cola Bottling of Corinth, the distributor for the Batesville area, provided financial support for the art students. Two local companies provided the highlift unit and other needed equipment, and Home Depot donated the paint.

Because the building on which the sign was painted was located close to a busy main street, the students were limited to painting only four hours per day. The lift unit blocked a portion of the street which required a police controlled detour to be in place from 10am until 2pm daily. The lift unit also was required to be removed and re-positioned each day.

Professor Bork had done extensive research to assure the paint colors to be used were identical to those in the original mural. The 30 x 90 foot sign is located on the side of Big's Restaurant, but when first painted in the 1920s it advertised the site of a grocery store. It became a Coca-Cola mural in the 1930's and changed to the Sprite Boy design in the 1940s.

Professor Bork had moved to Batesville ten years earlier and recalled at that time noting the mural's poor condition. He estimated that without the restoration by his students in 2019, the mural would have been completely lost in just a few more years.

Bork commented "the students really took ownership" of the project, and he was confident of their ability to paint their first large scale mural. The five students, working only limited hours each day, completed the project in one month.

A ribbon cutting ceremony to celebrate the restoration was held by the chamber of commerce in May 2019. A selfie star was placed on a nearby sidewalk and visitors were encouraged to use the mural as a photo backdrop.

Lyon College art students along with their professor restored the Sprite Boy mural. Left to right: Morgan Henson, Hayley Cormican, Victoria Hutcheson, Kacy Perkins, Dustyn Bork

Several art students said working on the mural for Coca-Cola had opened doors for them to other projects.

Victoria Hutcheson reported the experience and publicity received brought her a commission to do another large mural near her hometown in Missouri. Victoria, who is from East Prairie, was hired after graduation to design and paint a mural for the New Madrid Historical Museum. Located on an outside museum wall, the 40 x 11 foot painting provides views of significant times in the area's history.

The following year Victoria entered post graduate study at Florida State University in Tallahassee where she studied Art Therapy, the use of art in medical and emotional situations.

Professor Bork remembered Victoria as a "leader and organizer" during the Coca-Cola restoration project.

SOS - Albion, Michigan

The complete restoration of an old Coca-Cola mural played a major role in a downtown beautification project in Albion, Michigan. It is believed it was first painted in 1920 or earlier, and is considered to be one of the largest outdoor Coca-Cola murals. Even more unusual is the mural's unique location over a river.

The sign's site alongside and over the Kalamazoo River was first used in 1903 to advertise the Davis Piano Store, which occupied the lower level of the 2-story building. However, the river's great flood of 1908 did significant damage to the wall, and the piano store was forced to go out of business.

It was reported that for weeks after the flooding beautiful Chippendale pianos were seen floating for miles down the river. One surprised fisherman was reported to have said, "you can tune a piano, but you can't tuna fish."

Next to appear on the building's river wall location was the original Coca-Cola mural. The exact date when the sign was first painted is not certain, but the "relieves fatigue" message on the sign was used by Coca-Cola primarily between 1907 and 1912. That early sign remained untouched and deteriorating for thirty-six years until two community leaders decided to get the badly faded sign repainted.

Mary Moore and Polly Ballou, with promotional help from local publicist Linda Kolmodin, initiated a fund raising campaign to support their project. With half of the needed funds donated by the former Jackson Coca-Cola bottling company, the sign simply was repainted in 1983 without any surface restoration work being done.

The first restoration of the mural was completed in 1983.

A second "restore our Coke sign" fund raising effort began in September 2019 and within a year had exceeded its overall goal to "bring art and history to downtown Albion." In addition to the Coca-Cola mural restoration it then became possible to create a second mural on the Albion Ironworks building, which celebrated the long foundry history in the community, and a statue was erected which honored the founding of the sport of Tee-Ball in Albion.

Fund raising volunteer co-chair persons, Janet Domingo and Linda Kolmodin collected more than $50,000 in local donations, which then made it possible for the state's economic development corporation to add another $50,000. An additional $15,000 was jointly donated by the Coca-Cola Corporation and by Great Lakes Coca-Cola Bottling.

The complete restoration of the sign in the summer of 2020 presented rare challenges, and a firm specializing in conservation and historic preservation, located in nearby Saline, Michigan, was selected.

Because the mural had significantly deteriorated, more than just painting was required to save and preserve the sign and a process called "architectural conservation" was selected. Surface preparation and integrity, along with research to discover the true original colors and design were required. An additional challenge to the project was created by the sign's location over the Kalamazoo River as workers faced problems of access and the leeching of materials.

Ron Koenig

Few firms were available for the specialized restoration work, but the "Building Art and Conservation" corporation was located, and agreed to take on the project. Company owner Ron Koenig is an Architectural Conservator with over 25 years experience working on major historic restorations in several states. The firm specializes in cleaning, analyzing and stabilizing historic materials. Their work follows the tenets of the American Institute for Conservation.

The Albion sign work was performed in three stages; mural research and documentation, surface repair, and the restoration. A month was required for Koenig and his experienced workers to ultimately create an accurate historic mural, well preserved for future generations.

Historic preservation has become an important ingredient in Albion's renewed downtown development. An historic theatre has been restored and again is providing entertainment, a downtown museum was opened, and older buildings have been repurposed as new shops and businesses.

The citizens of Albion, like many others around the nation, made the decision to "save our sign" as an important memory in the city's history.

SOS - Cape Girardeau, Missouri

A mysterious Coca-Cola mural in Cape Girardeau, Missouri may be the only one of its kind ever to be painted. The unusual mural is located on a historic building which has mysteries of its own.

When first painted in the early 1900s the mural included the phrase "Relieves Fatigue," a slogan used often by Coca-Cola from 1907 to 1912. Included on the signs during those years was the price of 5-cents painted on each lower corner.

However at some time the sign in Cape Girardeau was repainted and the price on the

lower left corner was changed to read "3-cents plain." The reason for that one price change remains the mystery of the mural.

Cape Girardeau businessman David Knight bought the old building in 1974 and discovered the faded mural with the two different drink prices when the structure was being sandblasted.

The building, which had been abandoned for ten years, had been used for many purposes through the years and possibly one of those

uses created the need for the price change. Believed to have been built in 1939, the building first was a chandlery business to supply goods for the riverboats. It also served as a hotel, candy store, three different furniture stores, and a warehouse.

The building changed little despite occasional river flooding, including the historic flood of 1951 which crested at 41.8 feet. A flood wall, constructed in 1964, now is the site for numerous historic murals.

When Knight was remodeling the building to become a restaurant he made an interesting discovery. Hidden in the rafters on the third floor were about forty cases of

empty whiskey bottles, adding credence to one rumor of the building once being a brothel where bootleg liquor was bottled and sold during prohibition. An old exterior lift device might have been used to raise barrels of whiskey to the upper level bottling area. From that discovery speculation evolved that a 5-cents Coca-Cola drink might have included a little something extra.

A milder pricing theory from a local historian was that the more expensive Coca-Cola contained flavor choices of cherry, vanilla or even chocolate. Others think the 5-cents drink was served with ice while the other drink was not. Researchers at the Coca-Cola archives in Atlanta were unable to discover any historical information concerning a mural having two different drink prices. However they did suggest another possible explanation that a 3-cents plain was simply a serving of only the Coca-Cola syrup, while the more expensive choice was a fountain made glass of Coca-Cola. The researchers explained that consumers had been able to purchase just the syrup at some locations "well into the 50's".

After the old mural was uncovered Knight was approached by a representative of Coca-Cola who said the sign was historic and asked Knight to participate in the cost of restoration. He agreed and the work was done in 1978 with Coca-Cola and the local distributor also sponsoring the project.

Knight sold his restaurant, along with its legends and mysteries, to another area businessman in 1988, and the Port Cape Girardeau restaurant is now

part of what is called Warehouse Row, the city's historic district. As an important part of the river town's past, the area was nominated for listing on the National Register of Historic Places. Coca-Cola was first bottled in Cape Girardeau in 1917 by W.E. McCarty who also owned Coca-Cola Bottling of Cairo, Illinois. The Cape Girardeau business was sold in 1925 to Milde Bottling Works of Jackson, Missouri. Owners A. D. Milde and J.R. Hoffman had a third plant in Charleston.

Milde Bottling started as a soda water bottler in Jackson in 1894. Af-

ter buying the Coca-Cola plant they purchased another Cape Girardeau bottling company from Arthur Thilenius. His family had started the business in 1898, and Arthur then became manager of Milde's plant. A new $40,000 plant was constructed in 1941, and Thilenius purchased the business two years later.

Bottling was stopped in Cape Girardeau in 1969 due to a merger with the Jackson plant, and finally the sale of the entire business to Coca-Cola. The territory became Heartland Coca-Cola in 2017 when the franchise was acquired by former Milwaukee Bucks NBA star Junior Bridgeman.

Dale Clarke, general manager for Heartland's Jackson and Duquoin operations, has a drawing of the unique Cape Girardeau mural hanging in his office. He too believes the 5-cents Coca-Cola was simply one served with ice.

SOS - Union City, Georgia

It's the old and the new as a restored Coca-Cola mural and one of the nation's newest and most modern Coca-Cola sales and distribution centers reflect the growth and bright future for Union City, Georgia.

The 9-by-15 foot mural was first painted in the 1940's on the side of a pharmacy building. The sign was restored to observe the city's 110th anniversary in August 2018.

Mayor Vance Williams had been concerned about the badly faded mural since first becoming a city council member, and the restoration was discussed for

Mural being restored by William Mitchell of Atlanta. His business, "Squared Away Sign Company" has painted other murals for the Coca-Cola company.

Completed mural on the side of the city owned building.

several years. The new sign includes the phrase "Welcome to Union City" and it is positioned near a companion festival sign.

Ultimately the city purchased the old pharmacy building to renovate it and make a new home for the community development program. The mayor has urged the city to purchase other downtown buildings and use them to encourage new businesses to locate there.

The mural restoration was done by Coca-Cola Bottling Company United which at the same time was completing construction of a nearby sales and distribution center, to become one of the largest and most technologically advanced in the nation. The 450,000 square foot facility officially opened during a ceremony January 31, 2020. The $86 million investment required over 700 employees to serve more than 10,000 customers throughout the Atlanta area. It was estimated the new center would handle 36 million cases of beverages per year.

Coca-Cola Bottling Company United is the second largest privately held Coca-Cola bottler in North America. Headquartered in Birmingham, Alabama the company has 10,000 employees in 60 facilities throughout six southeastern states. United acquired the Atlanta territory from the Coca-Cola Company in 2017, and it is the largest single market in United's territory with two production and 10 sales centers. Construction for the Union City center began in early 2018 and was completed by the end of 2019. It is one of the largest Coca-Cola sales centers in the U.S.

SOS - North Branch, Minnesota

A badly faded Sprite Boy mural on the main street had become an eyesore to the residents of North Branch, Minnesota. The sign had weathered to the point where the image was almost not visible, and the local beautification association decided it was time to do something about it. No one was sure when the mural was first painted, but the Sprite Boy image had been used by Coca-Cola for only a few years starting in 1940.

Association President Christine Larson said it took about three years to arrange for the mural restoration and to gain community support and funding for the project which was completed in the fall of 2017. The association had estimated the cost to restore the sign would be about $1800, and an anonymous donation in that amount was received.

However after locating a professional painter it was learned at least another $1200 would be required. An additional $1,000 was then contributed by Viking Coca-Cola's North Branch operation, with another $200 being donated by Darrin Carlson, Viking's president of sales and marketing. Carlson was born and raised in North Branch having graduated from high school there in 1990. He said he was proud to support the restoration of the iconic sign which brought

back many memories from previous times in his hometown.

During the unveiling of the finished mural it was revealed that the initial contribution for the project had been made by Mike and Barbara Nelson who also were members of the association. Like Darrin Carlson they too grew up in North Branch and said they were proud of work being done by the Beautification Association and wanted to see the efforts continue.

The sign restoration was done by Toni Stafki, a professional artist whose Minneapolis business "Walls of Art" specializes in mural creation and restoration.

The North Branch mural is located on the upper portion of a two story building which at that time housed a business called The Cutting Zone. Glen Boyce, a retired attorney who owned an adjacent building, remembered that a variety of businesses had occupied the neighboring structure through the years, which added to the historical importance of both the building and the Coca-Cola mural.

SOS - Lost and Found: Two Georgia Signs

FOUND

It was a Coca-Cola sign found, and workmen were surprised when they uncovered the fifty-year-old mural in Hahira, Georgia. They were removing decorative wooden siding which had been added to an old commercial building on main street.

Records show the structure was built in 1900 for a corner grocery store. It was an office for a construction company when the siding was removed in 2018. Through the years the building also had been home for a five and ten cent store, and for an insurance company. The siding had been placed on the building in the 1980's. The Coca-Cola mural had been painted about ten years earlier and the siding, while hiding the sign, may also have helped preserve it.

Hahira's downtown development agency was coordinating efforts to restore the downtown area with the objective of becoming listed in the National Historic Register.

LOST

We can't save them all, but maybe we should or at least that's the goal of many organizations and historians, because the old Coca-Cola murals are more than just a form of advertising. Most of them are original works of art done by a sign artist with the basics of a brush, paint and a

ladder. They also serve as visual records of history often reflecting a time of life in America.

An incident in Valdosta, Georgia in 2020 is an example of how a valuable Coca-Cola mural and its message can be lost forever. The sign had been painted between 1904 and 1907 on a downtown building which was constructed in 1885.

Ironically in the 1890's before the sign was painted, the building had been the home for Valdosta Bottling Works, believed to be the second bottler in the nation to bottle Coca-Cola. The first was Joe Biedenharn in Vicksburg, Mississippi. Valdosta Bottling also sold several other soda flavors including Delaware Punch and NuGrape.

However, the Valdosta bottler had already moved to a different location when the Coca-Cola mural was painted. The sign, painted on an outside wall, remained exposed to the weather for about twenty years until an adjacent building was constructed and completely covered the mural. The new structure became the location for a Marmon auto dealership.

The sign was uncovered and partially damaged when a demolition crew was tearing down three buildings to create space for a planned hotel and event facility.

When the sign was revealed the nearby Lowndes County Historical Society and Museum was alerted. Additional demolition was halted for the day to allow museum Executive Director Donald Davis time to capture photos for the museum's records. The museum located just two blocks away, has been recognized for its extensive research on area Coca-Cola history.

SOS - *Nova Scotia, Canada*

Coca-Cola is sold and bottled world-wide, and the first place outside the United States where Coca-Cola was bottled was Canada in 1905.

A large outdoor Coca-Cola sign in Nova Scotia is believed to be one of the oldest in Canada, and clearly illustrates how Coca-Cola advertising remains the same everywhere. The mural has been restored several times since first painted in the early 1900s. It is 25-feet high and 40-feet wide and located on the historic Blanchard Building in downtown Windsor, where it was restored again in July 2020.

Top: Painter Markus Gallant. Photos courtesy of Carole Morris-Underhill/Hants Journal

The building's owner Rick Dunham noticed the mural had become badly faded from years of exposure to the weather. He said he believed it was his civic duty to restore the sign instead of having it painted over or sandblasted from the side of his building. He decided to pay for the restoration work calling the sign "an iconic mural which adds to the beautification of downtown."

Local painters Sean Arthur and Markus Gallant were hired for the $7500 project. The two are experienced interior and exterior building painters, but revitalizing the large mural was a first for them. The sign is on the second level of the building, about 30-feet off the ground which required the use of a lift unit by the painters. Gallant said their work received "lots of positive feedback" from passing viewers.

The phrase "Delicious and Refreshing" on the sign was used by Coca-Cola as early as 1900. The sign previously was refurbished in 1999 and the sign painter at that time quickly noticed something wrong as the sign's background had been painted green.

While repainting the downtown Windsor sign, Ken Spearing corrected the background changing it from green to red.

Nova-Scotian artist Ken Spearing knew it should have been a bright red, and as he prepared the surface for his work he removed layers from previous paint jobs to uncover the exact red color he would use. Ken believed the previous green background could be attributed to a color mistake in an old photo which the painter had used as a guide. The Coca-Cola Company of Canada, which had hired Spearing, was pleased to see the sign returned to it's original color. Spearing also restored another ghost mural in Windsor which

had been painted on the side of a furniture manufacturing building. The unusual sign included the phrase "Made in Canada."

Coca-Cola of Canada is an independent family owned bottler which started in a small plant in Toronto in 1905. The company now has facilities in every province including more than fifty sales and distribution centers and five manufacturing plants.

SOS - Kilgore, Texas

A large Coca-Cola mural in Kilgore, Texas has become one of the city's most visited sites. It's recognized as a "must do" selfie stop for Kilgore visitors, while the locals often use the sign as a favorite backdrop to create special memories such as the high school prom, senior photos or sports awards. It's recognized as one of

the most photographic locations in Kilgore.

The sign originally was painted on the outside wall in the 1950s when the building served as the city's post office. The structure has been owned for over 70 years by Bobby Speer and his family and now houses the BTH Bank.

Speer had the sign touched up in the 1960s and hired a local painter to do the work. He said Coca-Cola was not interested in saving the sign when he contacted them first about doing the restoration.

The mural includes two large Coca-Cola bottle images which the company started featuring in many signs as early as 1924. It was intended to continue recognition of the exclusive bottle which was designed during a bottle manufacturers' competition initiated in 1905 by the Coca-Cola company.

It's not certain who was first responsible for painting the large sign in Kilgore as Coca-Cola was never bottled there. However, in the early 1900's three other nearby east Texas towns had bottling plants. Marshall was first in 1908 followed by Tyler in 1909 and then Longview in 1912.

The old building where the sign is located has historical significance of its own because of its design and for serving as the Kilgore post office for many years. Consideration was being given to having the structure registered as a historic site.

Vintage Coca-Cola murals have become popular attractions in many cities, and in Kilgore it's not uncommon to hear someone suggest "let's go to the Coke sign."

SOS
Sign To Be Saved In West Virginia

An old Coca-Cola mural became an unexpected addition to an expanding historical district in Point Pleasant, West Virginia. The mural was uncovered in 2020 on an old commercial building when the adjacent property was being cleared for construction of the city's new River Museum.

The site included an old theater and a collapsed former bar building, while the neighboring structure holding the Coca-Cola mural had been built for a hardware store and barber shop in 1895. Recently it housed the former Harris Steak House.

The River Museum had been located just a few blocks away, also on Main Street, but had sustained damage during a recent fire, and because of the building's

age it was decided to build at a new location. The original museum building had been built in 1854 as a mercantile to serve nearby Ohio River traffic. After the fire consideration was given to destroying the damaged building, but another local organization, The Mason County Historical and Preservation Society stepped in to save, renovate and move into the former museum, creating another historical attraction for the area.

The Society also became interested in the newly discovered Coca-Cola sign, and spokesman Chris Rizer said they would save the sign along with two other historically significant city murals. Point Pleasant's Main Street Program was to assist in the mural project.

The badly faded phrase on the mural is "Drink Coca-Cola, Delicious and Refreshing," which according to Coca-Cola archives indicated the sign was painted in the 1930s. It probably was paid for by the Coca-Cola Bottling Company of Point Pleasant which began business in 1917 and was an active bottler in the 1930s. The mural was painted by the R. C. Maxwell Company which was founded in 1894 in New Jersey and created large signs throughout the United States for over one-hundred years. The location for the mural may have been selected because of the adjacent bar and a nearby hotel.

After the mural was discovered the Society then had to determine how it would be preserved; to restore it or to simply apply a clear coating to maintain the sign's original design. Rizer said all three city murals are "beautiful relics of the past" and needed to be saved to be appreciated by tourists and future generations.

Rizer indicated the society planned to consult with well known mural artist Robert Dafford from Louisiana to help decide on the best plan to preserve the sign. Dafford previously created a 150-ft long river wall in Point Pleasant. Coca-Cola enthusiasts also are familiar with Dafford's river wall creations in the historic Coca-Cola cities of Vicksburg, Mississippi and Paducah, Kentucky as each mural includes a section reflecting on that area's Coca-Cola history.

Robert Dafford mural wall along the river in Point Pleasant.

Chapter 25
Norton, Virginia

The memories of a former Coca-Cola plant shine brightly again in Norton, Virginia thanks to the efforts of city officials who sought support for their restoration project from a nearby Coca-Cola bottler. The project focused on an unusual old Coca-Cola neon sign which featured a large lighted clock on top. The large sign is 10.75 ft wide and just over 9 ft high. The sign was built in 1936 and for years was a reliable "time piece" for Norton residents. But the years and weather had taken a toll, and some described the sign as an "eyesore".

Photo by Will Bouton

City Manager Fred Ramey contacted Coca-Cola Consolidated in Charlotte for about five years before the large bottler finally agreed to take on the restoration. Consolidated had been involved for several years in a "ghost sign" restoration program which focused on restoring old outdoor wall murals.

The uniqueness of a sign with a large clock, along with the sign's prominent location, helped to gain the company's interest. A company spokesman said the Norton sign became the first metal sign to be revamped in their old sign project.

The Kinsey Neon & Sign Company of Roanoke completed the month long restoration in 2019. At a city celebration, Manager Ramey proclaimed the new sign to be a fitting tribute to the city's 125th anniversary. He noted that bottling is an important part of Norton's history, as the city had as many as three bottling plants in the early years.

Coca-Cola came to Norton after a franchise for

Participating in new sign celebration: Darryl Thompson, Kinsey Sign Company; Dr. Jeremiah Sturgill, building owner; Fred Ramey, City Manager; Blair Belk, Coca-Cola Consolidated; Joseph Fawbush, Mayor.

the entire Bristol area was granted in 1904 to Milton Rush. Norton is about 34 miles northwest of Bristol, Tennessee with area distribution being made by Dixie Bottling Works of Bristol.

Dixie Bottling was purchased in 1906 by Col. Sewell Howard of Rockwood, Tennessee, and he decided to build a new bottling plant in Bristol. The plant's older bottling equipment was moved to Norton where Sewell established Coca-Cola Bottling Works Inc. The Norton plant began operation in 1907 with Jack Tarwater listed as president. Tarwater was married to Sewell's daughter.

The Norton plant was purchased ten years later by F.B. Kline, who

Photo courtesy of Bristol Historical Association

Photo courtesy of Bristol Historical Association

built a newer facility on 7th street. Kline also owned another commercial building at 615 Park avenue, which is the location for the unusual neon clock sign. It is believed Kline selected that building for his sign as Park avenue is considered Norton's main street. In 2019 the building was an office for an orthodontist.

Photo courtesy of Bristol Historical Association

The sign was constructed in Chicago by Federal Sign Company, which in those days was producing numerous large outdoor and indoor signs for Coca-Cola. The sign was shipped to Norton by rail and installed by local workers. The Coca-Cola Bottling Company of Norton expanded in St. Paul, Virginia in the 1940's and into Vansant in 1949. The bottler also produced other soda

products including Superior brand ginger ale and sparkling water, and a line of of their own beverages called Lonesome Pine. They also were listed as a distributor for Budweiser beer.

Kline died in 1970 and his son William Armistead inherited part ownership and took over the operation of the company. Armistead finally sold the business and territory to Coca-Cola Consolidated. Kline's first Norton Coca-Cola plant, located on 7th street, remained and was being used for storage in 2019.

Meanwhile in Bristol, a million dollar Coca-Cola plant was built and opened for the public to view in March 1951. The new plant could produce 4,000 cases of Coca-Cola per day, and utilized a fleet of 26 trucks to serve over 2700 dealers in the area.

Coca-Cola Consolidated announced in July 2018 plans to close the Bristol plant and merge it with their operation in Johnson City, about 21 miles away. The move was completed in about three months, and fifty of

the sixty Bristol employees were transitioned to Johnson City.

The empty Bristol Coca-Cola building was purchased by local businessman Allen Harley, but plans for the building's future use were not revealed.

Chapter 26
Along The Trail
Arlington, Texas

It's a place where Coca-Cola and Texas bar-b-que meet. It's called "Cokers" and when you step inside you'll quickly know why. Restaurant customers are amazed by the amount of real Coca-Cola memorabilia on display.

Opened in Arlington, Texas in 1992 by a dedicated Coca-Cola memorabilia collector, Butch Donahower who envisioned it as the perfect place to feature two of his favorite pleasures, collecting Coca-Cola and Texas bar-b-que. He had been a serious memorabilia collector for fourteen years.

Although Butch died about ten years after opening the business, his Coca-Cola collection still is being enjoyed at Cokers located at 2612 W. Pioneer Parkway. Butch's business partner and friend continued the restaurant which has become a popular area attraction.

"Dimebag Darrell" the co-founder and guitarist for the heavy metal band Pantera decided the food at Cokers was his favorite

and it was often catered for the band's backstage enjoyment or for his own birthday parties.

It's not unusual for a restaurant customer to offer to purchase one or more of the displayed Coca-Cola items. The offers are politely refused, but the customer is able to select from a full menu of traditional Texas bar-b-que accompanied by a large side of Coca-Cola memories.

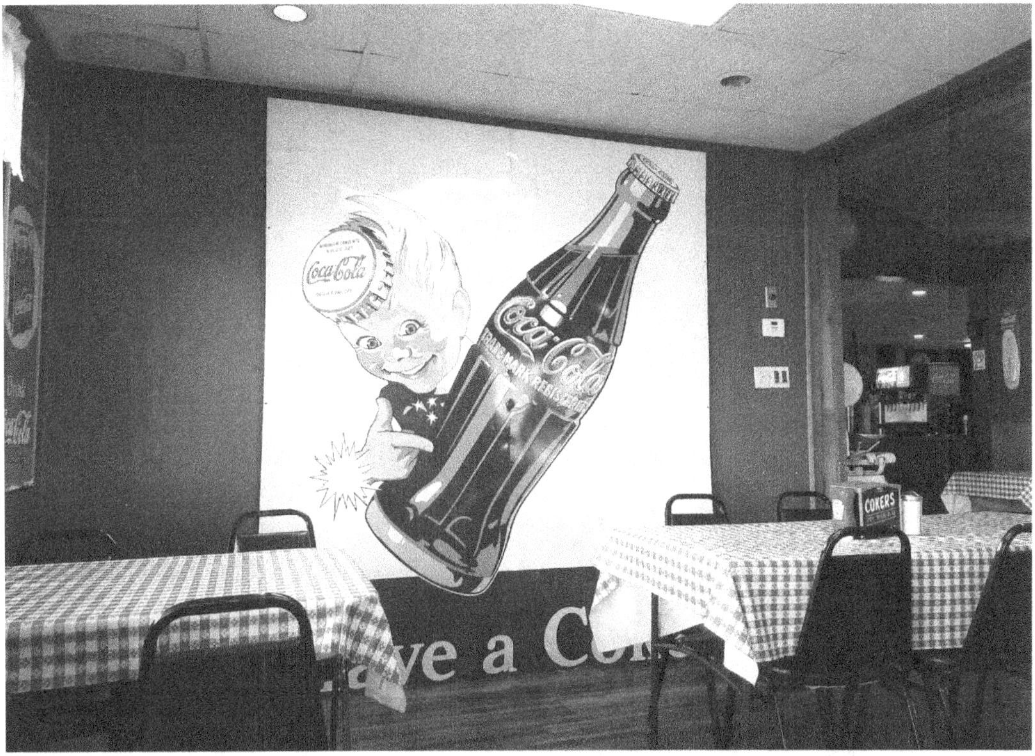
Coca-Cola
Coca-Cola
COKERS

Coke is it!
Coca-Cola REFRESHING
DALLAS
COWBOYS
Coca-Cola
ICE COLD
Coca-Cola

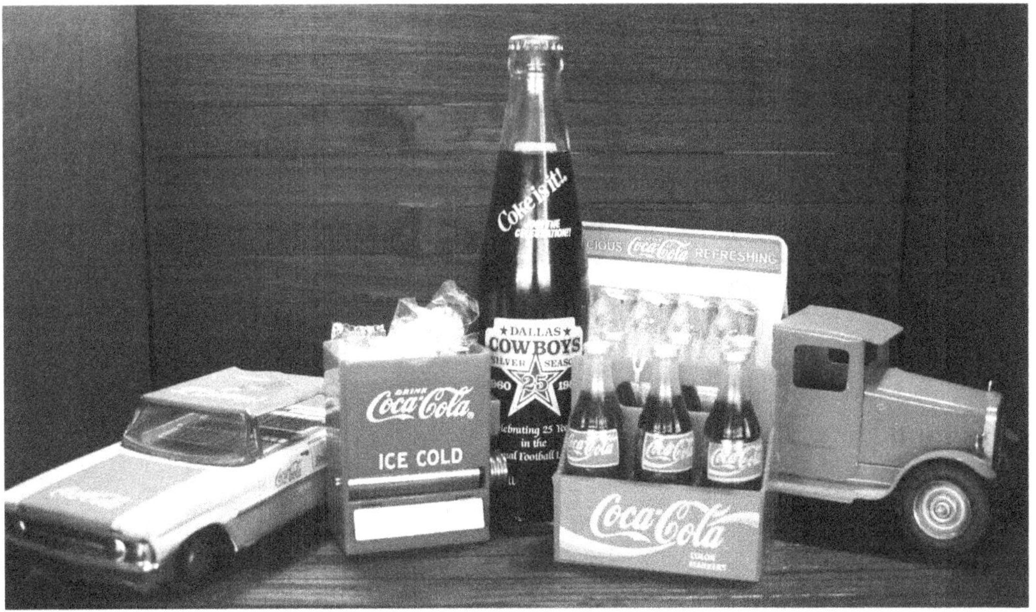

Galveston, Texas

The oldest drug store in Texas also proudly displays the state's oldest working Coca-Cola neon sign. It's located in Galveston on the front of the Star Drug Store, one of two buildings constructed in 1886 by the Scanlons, a prominent real estate family.

The building has survived gulf storms and even fire during its more than 230 years, and has remained as first designed by Nicholas Clayton a renowned early Galveston architect.

The basic structure was changed from wood to brick when purchased in 1906 by a local druggist. A popular horseshoe shaped soda fountain was added in 1917. The distinctive Coca-Cola neon sign was created and installed in the 1940s by Jules Lauve, Jr, who created unique signs and billboards for over 50 years in the Galveston area.

Friday the 13th in March of 1998 proved to be an "unlucky day" for Star Drug Store when a major fire forced it to be closed with an uncertain future. However, three years later the Tilts family purchased the badly damaged structure and began the restoration which would return it to the

Photo courtesy of Galveston Daily News

original appearance and reopen a treasured Galveston memory. The Coca-Cola neon sign had been kept in safe storage and was installed again to be able to shine when customers returned.

The old store withstood one more tragedy in September 2008 when hurricane "Ike" delivered a devastating blow to Galveston. Over six feet of flood water seriously damaged the store's furnishings, equipment and inventory resulting in another temporary closure.

The famous Coca-Cola signed survived the storm's fury, and with the help of friends, family and employees the store reopened and the sign glowed again in less than three months.

Along with a Coca-Cola, a homemade hamburger or other menu item, visitors to Star Drug in Galveston are treated to a special history shared by friendly store employees.

Corinth, Mississippi

When the Coca-Cola Trail takes you back to Corinth in northern Mississippi you will find a new Coca-Cola museum and what may be one of the most unique selfie signs ever created. The "Trails" initial visit to Corinth in our first book details the fascinating history of a family dedicated to the business of Coca-Cola since 1907.

This second visit to Corinth discovers a brand-new Coca-Cola museum located across the street from the Coca-Cola headquarters at 601 Washington Street. It is the second time Corinth Coca-Cola has created a public museum with the first being opened in 2007 as part of the company's 100th anniversary celebration.

A flood three years later seriously damaged the museum building forcing it to be closed. Much of the museum's collection was put back on

Corinth Coca-Cola Museum

temporary display about a year later at the city's Crossroad Museum. However, some items were placed in storage until the new museum was opened in the summer of 2017. Displayed there are over 1,000 pieces of authentic Coca-Cola memorabilia including a large variety of old vending machines.

"A Coke and A Smile" may be the slogan which comes to mind at the next Corinth stop on the trail. A clever selfie sign painted on the outside wall of a historic downtown building features a hand slowly pouring Coca-Cola from a large bottle. The unique sign becomes interactive when the person having their photo taken appears to be enjoying a drink from the slightly tilted bottle. Foot print marks on the ground in front of the sign show exactly where to stand to create the one-of-a-kind Coca-Cola Corinth souvenir.

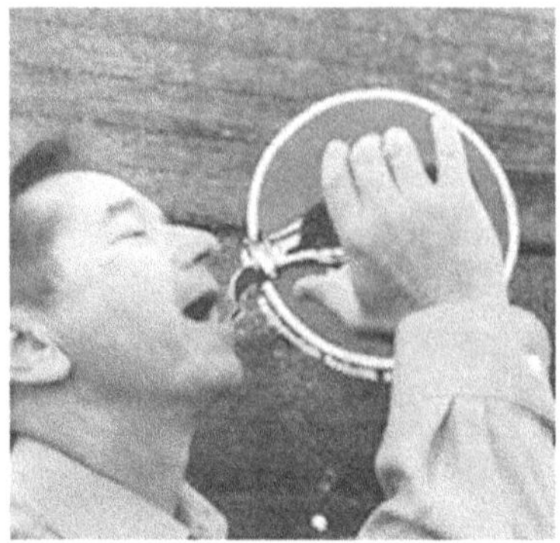

A veteran Coca-Cola employee from Atlanta, Dan Markle tried out the unique selfie and left impressed during his recent "retirement visit" to Corinth. Dan had been with Coca-Cola for 37 years and no doubt the photo will be a special memory.

The city planned to add a small park area in front of the mural with benches and a community-wide bulletin board giving the location the name of "Corinth Connection Park". The creative mural wall was inspired by Corinth's rich Coca-Cola history.

Historic Country Store

Buchanan's Store by Mark Ray

Coca-Cola fans and memorabilia collectors who enjoy old photos and paintings will treasure the painting of the oldest family owned country store in the southeastern United States. Created by artist Mark Ray the painting depicts Buchanan's store in Manson, North Carolina. Opened April 13, 1878 by the Buchanan brothers the store remains under the ownership of the Buchanan family.

Photo by June Banks Evans

Mark Ray is a well-known fish and wildlife artist and photographer working from his home studio in White Oak, Ohio. He created the painting of the Buchanan store as a special project for a friend, and explained it is not his "normal subject matter." His painting has been reproduced and became available on prints and other souvenir items for the historic store.

The store was opened to meet the early days needs of the area's rural families, and also served for several years as the official location for the Warren County York post office. The store soon became a community gathering place where farmers would discuss the weather and compare tobacco prices and where neighbors would meet for annual Christmas parties and other social activities.

The official ledger from the store's first day of business shows the sale of five fish hooks for four cents. Fishing needs remain a popular item today with Kerr Lake located about fifty miles away on the North Carolina-Virginia border. The 50,000-acre lake was created between 1947 and 1952 by damming the Roanoke River to produce hydroelectricity. With 850 miles of shoreline the lake is enjoyed by visitors and lake home owners for fishing, water sports, camping and other recreational activities.

The store's inventory has changed thru the years to meet changing needs of new customers. Among the current popular items are North Carolina products like jams, honey, peanut butter and unique artisan souvenirs along with always a good supply of cold Coca-Cola. The operators of the store since 2015 Jennie and Jamie Reese also added an ice cream bar

featuring shakes, sundaes, and homemade sandwiches.

The last Buchanan to actually manage the store was Robert Lee Buchanan in 1935, but the store remains owned by the Buchanan family, and current owners Lucy Buchanan "Cookie" Currin and her husband Earl Currin live nearby. Lucy is the granddaughter or Robert Lee Buchanan and proudly explains her grandfather was named Robert Lee because his father was a Confederate soldier in the Civil War.

The store is not exactly in its original location because in 1948 when the state paved and widened the road, the entire store was moved back several yards.

The image of the store attracted another painter back in 2002 when North Carolina's Rural Center recognized the store as one of two scenes which were representative of the state's rural counties. A watercolor painting done by the late artist Bob Pittman is displayed at the Rural Center offices in Raleigh. Pittman, who died in 2016, was one of the state's

Buchanan's Store by Bob Pittman

Photo by June Banks Evans

most admired artists and had painted hundreds of land and seascapes of
North Carolina.

The Buchanan store has received other recognition in recent years
as well, including a 2009 feature article in North Carolina Magazine and
special television attention in 2010 from WRAL-TV in Raleigh.

The store's owners will tell visitors the Buchanan Store remains a
"strong survivor in a time of super stores and quick marts because of the
charm of the past along with present day amenities."

Along The Trail - Bunkie, Louisiana

A new Coca-Cola sign made to look old and a Coca-Cola soda fountain greet visitors at an antique store and market place in Bunkie, Louisiana. The clever sign was created in the summer of 2020 by local artist Donna Laborde after she decided to open the store in a century old building which had been closed and empty for twenty years.

The sign is painted on what appears to be an inside brick wall at the store's entrance area. However, the wall actually is simply made of wood panels and the artist transformed the 8 x 20-foot surface into "faux" brick with a well-worn appearance.

Donna Laborde

To create the unique sign layers of plaster were first applied to form the final textured brick appearance. Narrow runners of tape were placed under the plaster which were removed after the plaster dried to give the look of cement between the bricks. The Coca-Cola logo was then added and also painted to look old and worn.

Store visitors also will enjoy a 50s style juke box and a drink from the Coca-Cola soda fountain. Memorabilia fans and treasure hunters have a lot to choose from in the two-story, ten-thousand square feet of dealer displays.

Coca-Cola has a long history in the central Louisiana town, as it was first bottled there in 1912. Clarence Joseph Pope owned the Bunkie Ice Company and had a personal friendship with the Biedenharns of Vicksburg who were the very first bottlers of Coca-Cola. The new soft drink was an excellent addition to Pope's business as he also was producing other carbonated flavors and "Honey Boy" ice cream.

He received a larger territory franchise for Coca-Cola in 1936 and the following year constructed the large bottling building which remains today just two blocks south of the antique mall on Main street. The plant was in operation

Original Bunkie Coca-Cola Bottling plant

until 1990 when the business was sold to Coca-Cola bottling of Alexandria which at that time was owned by the Biedenharn Coca-Cola bottling company of Monroe.

Since then the old Bunkie bottling building has been occupied by several local businesses, and although it has aged thru the years it maintains that classic style of those early years Coca-Cola plants.

Where did those magnificent machines come from?

Through the years, the challenge of powered transportation in the snow has been met with ideas from explorers, creative inventors and small companies, all with new ideas—often unique and sometimes successful. The name "snowmobile" was trademarked in 1917, but there were snow travel ideas before that date and certainly thousands more since.

Winter explorers and trailblazers sought to replace their dogsleds and snowshoes as they explored difficult locations, including remote locations, on the north and south poles. Early inventors of snow vehicles often scavenged parts from many mechanical devices, trying many power and propulsion methods, from 2- and 4-stroke engines to air propulsion, and even a "snow biting" screw auger concept.

The snow travel ideas from some early inventors were simply designed to solve their own needs; others came from entrepreneurs who believed folks would be impressed and want to buy their creations. Some of their ideas evolved into companies such as Polaris, Arctic Cat and Ski-Doo, which prospered and now can trace their roots back to that first snowmobile idea.

Make It Go In The Snow provides a fun look at the history of a few of the many thousands of snow travel ideas and those enthusiasts who gave them birth. Captured and recorded are a wide variety of snowmobile ideas, without offering judgment on any individual venture. Join me as I pay tribute to all those ideas; past, present and future. But keep watching, because more snow excitement is waiting to be created.

From Modern History Press

ISBN 978-1-61599-814-2